KANT'S
GROUNDWORK FOR THE METAPHYSICS OF MORALS

Continuum Reader's Guides

Aristotle's Nicomachean Ethics – Christopher Warne

Heidegger's Being and Time – William Blattner

Hobbes' Leviathan – Laurie Bagby

Hume's Enquiry Concerning Human Understanding – Alan Bailey and Dan O'Brien

Hume's Dialogues Concerning Natural Religion – Andrew Pyle

Nietzsche's Genealogy of Morals – Daniel Conway

Plato's Republic – Luke Purshouse

Wittgenstein's Tractatus-Logico Philosophicus – Roger M.White

KANT'S
GROUNDWORK FOR THE
METAPHYSICS OF MORALS

A Reader's Guide

PAUL GUYER

continuum

Continuum International Publishing Group
The Tower Building   80 Maiden Lane
11 York Road   Suite 704
London SE1 7NX   New York, NY 10038

British Library Cataloging-in-Publication Data
A catalogue record for this book is available from the British Library.

ISBN: HB: 0826484530
9780826484536
PB: 0826484549
9780826484543

Library of Congress Cataloguing-in-Publication Data
A catalog record for this book is available from the Library of Congress.

Typeset by Servis Filmsetting Ltd, Manchester

Printed and bound in Great Britain by
MPG Books Ltd, Bodmin, Cornwall

CONTENTS

SOURCES AND ABBREVIATIONS

All citations and references to Kant's works are located by volume and page number as in *Kant's gesammelte Schriften*, edited by the Royal Prussian (later German, then Berlin-Brandenburg) Academy of Sciences (Berlin: Georg Reimer, later Walter de Gruyter & Co., 1900–), the so-called 'Academy Edition' of Kant's works. The one exception to this rule is the *Critique of Pure Reason*, where passages are located by page numbers from 'A,' the first edition of 1781, and/or 'B,' the second edition of 1787. The Academy Edition page numbers and the 'A' and 'B' page numbers of the *Critique of Pure Reason* are provided in all modern editions and translations.

In the Academy Edition, the *Groundwork for the Metaphysics of Morals* (abbreviated as *G*, though the abbreviation will usually be omitted) is found in volume 4 (1911), pp. 385–463, and was edited by Paul Menzer. However, I have based my translations of passages from the *Groundwork* on the recent edition Immanuel Kant, *Grundlegung zur Metaphysik der Sitten*, edited by Bernd Kraft and Dieter Schönecker (Hamburg: Felix Meiner Verlag, 1999).

Translations from the *Critique of Practical Reason* (abbreviated as *PracR*) and the *Metaphysics of Morals* (abbreviated *MM*) are from Immanuel Kant, *Practical Philosophy*, edited and translated by Mary J. Gregor (Cambridge: Cambridge University Press, 1996).

Translations from the *Critique of Pure Reason* (abbreviated as *PureR*) are from Immanuel Kant, *Critique of Pure Reason*, edited and translated by Paul Guyer and Allen W. Wood (Cambridge: Cambridge University Press, 1998).

Translations from Immanuel Kant, *Religion within the Boundaries of Mere Reason* (abbreviated *Religion*) are from Immanuel Kant, *Religion and Rational Theology*, edited and translated by Allen W. Wood and George di Giovanni (Cambridge: Cambridge University Press, 1996).

Translations from Kant's notes in Chapter 2 are from Immanuel Kant, *Notes and Fragments*, edited by Paul Guyer, translated by Curtis Bowman, Paul Guyer, and Frederick Rauscher (Cambridge: Cambridge University Press, 2005).

The source for my translations of quotations from Kant's lectures on ethics is Immanuel Kant, *Vorlesung zur Moralphilosophie*, edited by Werner Stark (Berlin: Walter de Gruyter & Co., 2004).

The *Groundwork*, like all of Kant's works, was originally set in *Fraktur*, the traditional German typeface. *Fettdruck*, or larger and bolder type, was used for emphasis, and Roman type was reserved for foreign words (such as *a priori*). There was thus a typographical distinction between emphasis and foreign words in the original that would be lost if italics were used for both purposes in the translation, following normal, contemporary English practice. To avoid this, I have used boldface to reproduce Kant's *Fettdruck*, and italics to reproduce his Roman type.

CHAPTER 1

CONTEXT

1. KANT'S LIFE AND WORKS

Immanuel Kant's *Groundwork for the Metaphysics of Morals* (*Grundlegung zur Metaphysik der Sitten*), first published in 1785, remains after more than two centuries one of the most widely read works of Western philosophy. The *Groundwork* enjoys this status because of its striking thesis that the incomparable dignity and unconditional value of human autonomy is the necessary and sufficient condition of all morality, both that small part of morality which should be enforced by the coercive power of the state and the much larger part of morality which should be enforced only by the power of individual and societal conscience. Kant derives this idea from common-sense notions of good will and duty that he believes to be accessible to every normal human being, and then tries to support it with the abstruse and controversial metaphysics that he developed in his *magnum opus*, the *Critique of Pure Reason* (1781). Moreover, he attempts to do this in a very short work. Kant's exposition is thus dense and complex. For many readers, the attractiveness of Kant's central moral idea is also threatened by his metaphysical defense of it. For these reasons, the present work will ask whether the moral conception of Kant's *Groundwork* can stand without its metaphysical foundation.

Immanuel Kant (1724–1804) was the leading philosopher of the later phase of the Enlightenment in Germany. He was born and died in the East Prussian city of Königsberg (now Kaliningrad, Russia), and with the exception of a few years spent as a household tutor on several estates in its hinterlands, he spent his whole life there and his whole career in its university. Kant came from a family of very modest means, but his intellectual promise was noted early on by the family's Pietist pastor, and from ages eight to sixteen he received the best possible education the city had to offer at its leading school, which offered an intensive curriculum of Latin, Greek, Hebrew, French, mathematics, geography, and history.[1] At the university – where sixteen was not an unusually early age to start – Kant did not, as might have been expected of him, concentrate on theology, but instead pursued a diverse program of studies, continuing his work in Latin and mathematics while adding philosophy and physics. Although the Königsberg university was small, it had a talented faculty who exposed Kant to the most recent developments in natural philosophy as well as philosophy proper: thus Kant quickly imbibed Newton's physics, which would always remain his model of successful science, as well as the metaphysics of Germany's leading philosophers, Gottfried Wilhelm Leibniz and Christian Wolff, whose idea of a thoroughly rational and harmonious universe would ultimately be transformed by Kant from the result of divine creation into the product of human thought itself.[2] The work that Kant offered as a thesis for the *Magister* degree, the *True Estimation of Living Forces* (1747), which attempted to resolve a dispute between Cartesians and Leibnizians over the proper measurement of forces, anticipated his lifelong penchant for resolving philosophical debates by means of dialectical demonstrations that each side had part of the truth but neither side the whole truth. Unfortunately, the thesis was rejected, apparently not so much because the Frenchman Jean D'Alembert had already provided a better solution – a fact of which neither Kant nor his teacher Martin Knutzen seems to have been aware – but because Kant had earned Knutzen's disfavor by differing with him on another philosophical matter, the nature of the mind–body relation.[3] Kant left the university without a degree, and spent the years 1748 to 1754 as a private tutor – in any case not an uncommon way for eighteenth-century intellectuals without private means to begin their careers.

In 1754 Kant was able to return to Königsberg with a sheaf of scientific and philosophical writings in hand, which quickly earned him the master's degree, the doctor's degree, and the right to offer lectures as a *Privatdozent*, paid by the students taking his courses rather than by the university. The most important of these writings were the *Universal Natural History and Theory of the Heavens* and the *New Elucidation of the First Principles of Metaphysical*

Cognition, both published in 1755. In the first of these, Kant used Newtonian principles to explain how the solar system could have evolved from a nebular cloud of particles – what later became known as the Kant-Laplace hypothesis – while in the second he tentatively began the critique of both Cartesian and Leibnizo-Wolffian metaphysics that would become increasingly important to his philosophical work. It was in this work that Kant first rejected the famous ontological argument for the existence of God, which attempted to infer the existence of God from the concept of a perfect being, by arguing that existence can never be part of the content of a concept but is always an addition to that content. In order to make ends meet, Kant lectured on a wide range of subjects, not just logic, metaphysics, and ethics but also physics, physical geography, and subsequently anthropology; he also took a position as a university librarian. These duties naturally cut into the time he had for research and writing, and his next group of significant publications did not appear until 1762–4, when Kant published three important articles, including an 'Inquiry concerning the distinctness of the principles of natural theology and morality,' in which he insisted on the fundamental difference between the constructive method of mathematics and the analytical method of philosophy, and two books, the technical *Only Possible Argument in support of a Demonstration of the Existence of God* (1763), which extended his criticism of the traditional arguments for the existence of God while proposing an (ill-fated) argument of his own, and the popular *Observations on the Feeling of the Beautiful and Sublime* (1764), which anticipates more of his later anthropology than of his aesthetics. These were followed in 1766 by the *Dreams of a Spirit-Seer Elucidated by Dreams of Metaphysics*, in which Kant continued his attack upon rationalist metaphysics by comparing them to the fantasies of the Swedish spiritualist Emmanuel Swedenborg.

Kant spent fifteen years as an underpaid lecturer, but in 1770 was finally appointed to the salaried chair in Logic and Metaphysics.[4] On this occasion, Kant had to deliver and defend an inaugural dissertation, called *On the Form and Principles of the Sensible and Intelligible Worlds*, in which he argued that space and time are the forms of all of our experiences of things, but that the very fact that we know this to be necessarily true means that space and time are only features of the way we represent things, or their appearance, rather than features of things as they are in themselves, independently of our representation of them. This was the germ of the doctrine that Kant would later call 'transcendental idealism,' although at this stage Kant did not apply the theory to our general concepts such as substance and causation and held that these could yield knowledge of things as they are in themselves, including both God and our own souls. Kant's denial that space and time are features of things as they are in themselves met with incredulity then (as now). But the objections to this doctrine did not dissuade Kant. Rather, they started a long process of reflection which, after a 'silent decade' of non-publication, finally led to the monumental *Critique of Pure Reason* (1781), in which Kant extended rather than retrenched his transcendental idealism. Specifically, Kant argued that since general concepts like substance, causation, and interaction can only yield knowledge when applied to the representation of particular objects in space and time ('intuitions'), *all* of our knowledge is confined to the appearance of things rather than their reality; however, Kant also argued, precisely because our *cognitive* use of these concepts, above all the concept of universal causation, is limited to the *appearances* of things, we can at least *conceive* and *believe* that things as they are may be different than their appearances, specifically that at the level of reality rather than appearance there may be room for a belief in the freedom of our own wills and a divine plan for the world. It would then become one of the central themes of Kant's moral philosophy that we have moral or 'practical' grounds for such beliefs even though we do not have adequate cognitive grounds for them. In famous words from the preface to the second edition of the *Critique of Pure Reason*, Kant thus wrote that he had 'to deny **knowledge** in order to make room for **faith**' (B xxx).

Although Kant was already fifty-seven when he published the *Critique of Pure Reason*, for the next two decades his productivity was enormous. In 1783, the *Prolegomena to any Future Metaphysics that shall come forth as Scientific* attempted both to popularize and to defend the *Critique* from the opposition that it quickly encountered. In 1784, Kant published an important essay on 'The Idea of Universal History from a Cosmopolitan Point of View.' In 1785, he published the *Groundwork*. In 1786, he published the *Metaphysical Foundations of Natural Science*, which applied the basic principles of the *Critique of Pure Reason* to an empirical conception of matter in order to reconstruct Newtonian physics. This should have been followed by a *Metaphysical Foundations of Morals* that would apply the

4

basic principles of the *Groundwork* to basic empirical facts about the circumstances of human life in order to arrive at a specific doctrine of legal (coercively enforceable) and ethical (non-coercively enforceable) duties. But in 1787 Kant published a substantially revised edition of the *Critique of Pure Reason*, and his attempt to clarify his position on freedom of the will in that work led to a second critique in 1788, namely the *Critique of Practical Reason*. This was then followed in 1790 by a third critique, the *Critique of the Power of Judgment*, in which Kant treated the popular eighteenth-century topics of aesthetics and teleology within his own critical system, and in 1793 by *Religion within the Boundaries of Mere Reason*, in which Kant argued that all the central beliefs of Christianity could be reinterpreted as symbols of the central concepts of morality as he understood it (and also further revised his treatment of freedom of the will). After the important political tract *Toward Perpetual Peace* of 1795, in 1797 Kant finally did publish the *Metaphysics of Morals*, a detailed system of legal and ethical duties based on the central conception of the *Groundwork*. After his retirement that year, he published two more works, a handbook on *Anthropology from a Pragmatic Point of View* based on the lectures in that subject (really empirical psychology) that he had given since 1772, and the *Conflict of the Faculties*, a defiant brief for academic freedom. He spent his final years until his death in 1804 on an uncompleted restatement of his transcendental philosophy and philosophy of science, the manuscripts of which were eventually published under the name of the *Opus postumum*.

2. MORAL PHILOSOPHY IN THE TIME OF KANT

Let us now turn from Kant himself to the situation in moral philosophy that he encountered. The intellectual ferment of early modernity, that is, the movements we call the Renaissance, the Reformation and Counter-Reformation, and the Scientific Revolution, were accompanied with intense activity in moral philosophy. Many approaches were on offer. Traditionalists, especially but not exclusively Protestants, held to an ethics of divine command, or voluntarism: the theory going back to St. Augustine that actions are right or wrong simply because God has commanded their performance or omission, and that we should do as God wills in order to honor him, earn his rewards, and avoid his punishments. René Descartes, an unorthodox Catholic, even extended voluntarism to non-moral eternal truths, such as the truths of logic and mathematics. Others, including more progressive Protestants such as Hugo Grotius and Samuel Pufendorf, advocated the theory of natural law, which goes back at least to St. Thomas Aquinas: according to this theory, God wills that humans pursue their own well-being and has given them the faculty of reason so that they can figure out without his direct intervention the means He has created for them to realize this goal. Meanwhile, the revival of interest in ancient skepticism in response to doctrinal conflict among Christian sects – associated especially with Michel de Montaigne – led to an interest in other Hellenistic ethics as well, both Epicureanism and Stoicism; by the eighteenth century, the writings of Seneca and Cicero would become central to the education of every cultivated European. A theory of rational egoism, that is, that humans should use their faculty of reason to figure out what is in their own best interest but in so doing would realize that cooperation with others or even submission to a strongly coercive government would maximize their self-interest, was promulgated in the seventeenth century by Thomas Hobbes and renewed in the eighteenth century by Bernard Mandeville. In response, the theory of 'moral sense' was developed by Richard Cumberland, Anthony Ashley Cooper (the third Earl of Shaftesbury), Francis Hutcheson, and David Hume, according to which human beings are not motivated merely by self-interest but have a natural feeling of approbation toward benevolent actions and of abhorrence toward selfish ones – a disposition that may be a gift of God or Providence but does not presuppose any knowledge of God's will or commands. In eighteenth-century Germany, however, the prevailing theory, under the influence of Leibniz and Wolff, was a form of perfectionism, according to which the duty of human beings is to recognize the perfection of God and to reflect it in their own conduct by seeking to perfect the potentialities inherent in human nature.

Although it will be central to Kant's argument in the *Groundwork* that at some level every normal human being actually employs and therefore must at least tacitly know the fundamental principle of morality, Kant held that none of these moral *philosophies*, ancient or modern, had yet properly characterized this principle, its source, and the proper motivation for conforming to it. To put it bluntly, Kant held that the moral principles offered by these theories were

arbitrary or vacuous, and that what they counted as moral motivation was for the most part contemptible rather than noble. Kant
expressed these criticisms through a scheme that he frequently used
both in his published works and in his lectures on ethics. In the
Groundwork, Kant bases his critique on what we may call methodological or epistemological principles, in good part because he holds
that the methodological confusions of prior moral philosophers
prevented them from giving a clear substantive account of the fundamental principle of morality at all. He states that moral theories
have attempted to ground their principles either empirically or
rationally, that is, on experience or on *a priori* concepts (*G*, 4:441–2),
which are indeed the only possibilities for any theory-construction.
In the *Critique of Practical Reason*, Kant makes the same point by
dividing moral theories into 'subjective' and 'objective' ones (*PracR*,
5:40). Empirical or subjective theories have tried to derive moral
principles from the 'physical' feeling of happiness (Epicurus), from
a special 'moral feeling' (Hutcheson), or from conventions of education or government (Montaigne and Mandeville). But moral
feeling cannot be counted upon to lead to morally appropriate
conduct in all circumstances – sometimes sympathy is exactly the
wrong rather than the right response to the intentions of another –
while the pursuit of individual happiness or local customs can pretty
much be counted on to lead to moral conflicts in many situations,
when what would make me happy is precisely what would make you
unhappy. In other words, all of these theories leave moral principles
up to the '**particular arrangement of human nature** or to contingent
circumstances' (*G*, 4:442), and therefore cannot come up with a principle that is valid for all human beings at all places and times, let
alone valid for all rational beings as such (a requirement on which
Kant insists, though he never affirms that there *are* any rational
beings other than human beings). Moreover, there is nothing particularly noble about being motivated to act merely by an interest in
one's own happiness or by accidental circumstances of one's
upbringing or customs.

  Meanwhile, 'rational' or 'objective' theories have been vacuous or
question-begging. Kant holds that perfectionism has been 'empty'
and 'indeterminate' (*G*, 4:443), and can yield determinate principles
of action only if it presupposes an empirical conception of human
perfection or well-being (a fair criticism of Wolff's perfectionism).
A morality based on the principle that we should do what God

commands simply because of the perfection of his own will is even worse. First, it must tacitly presuppose that we have an antecedent knowledge of the principles of morality so that we can recognize that what purport to be divine commands really are such, and is thus circular. Second, it attributes to God himself a 'lust for glory and domination' and locates our own motivation to be moral in our 'fearful representations' of God's 'power and vengefulness,' which leads to a 'system of ethics that is diametrically opposed to morality' and makes our own motivation to do what is moral contemptible rather than admirable (4:442). In Kant's view, although this got him in trouble with the religious conservatives who dominated the Prussian government after the death of his patron Frederick the Great in 1786, theological ethics is thus both intellectually dishonest, because it presupposes that we know what is right and wrong antecedently to forming our conception of God's will, and mean, because it portrays us as motivated merely by the self-interested motives of love of reward or fear of punishment rather than by any genuine concern for other human beings. (Although Kant criticizes Wolff and Shaftesbury on other grounds, both of them had made a similar critique of theological ethics. Shaftesbury had put the point by saying that such theological ethics is 'mercenary' rather than 'disinterested,' thus a disguised form of rational egoism.)[5]

Kant was often friendlier to Epicureanism and Stoicism than to more modern moral philosophies. But he objected that neither adequately distinguished between virtue and happiness: Epicureanism failed to see that the pursuit of happiness, no matter how refined its conception of happiness is, is not in itself virtuous, while Stoicism failed to recognize that even the achievement of virtue does not by itself guarantee happiness in any ordinary sense. Thus, neither of these approaches realized that 'the maxims of virtue and those of one's own happiness are entirely heterogeneous as regards their highest practical principle' (*PracR*, 5:113).

Where does all this leave Kant? In his view, a fundamental principle of morality has to be truly universal, thus apply to all human beings regardless of time and place, indeed to all possible rational beings. Thus it must be known *a priori* rather than empirically, although it could not be known *a priori* by any of the means thus far canvassed. Moreover, genuinely moral motivation must be nobler than a mere desire for one's own happiness, thus than mere desire for reward and fear of punishment. Yet a moral theory that has nothing to say about happiness at all would be unrealistic, for human beings do naturally desire happiness and there is no reason for moral philosophy to neglect this fact altogether. Thus what Kant has to find is a genuinely universal principle of morality and a genuinely noble motivation to be moral, neither of which reduces morality to the pursuit of happiness, especially one's own happiness, but which do allow a proper concern for happiness within the framework of morality. This is Kant's task in the *Groundwork* and in his subsequent writings in moral philosophy.

CHAPTER 2

OVERVIEW OF THEMES

1. AUTONOMY AND MORALITY

How does Kant propose to answer the demands he has placed on a moral theory by his criticism of all previous theories? His proposal is that human reason itself commands us to achieve 'autonomy,' the 'quality of the will by means of which it is a law to itself (independently of any quality of the object of willing),' and that autonomy is equivalent to morality (*G*, 4:440). Part of the challenge in reading the *Groundwork*, however, is that although it is clearly based on the idea that human reason itself imposes the goal of autonomy, many of Kant's formulations of the fundamental principle of morality – or, more precisely, of the 'categorical imperative,' the form in which the universally valid and thus 'categorical' fundamental principle of morality presents itself to creatures like us, who are capable of recognizing and acting in accordance with it but also have inclinations in favor of actions that do not conform to it, and thus at least sometimes perceive it as a *constraint* or 'imperative' (*G*, 4:413–14) – do not use the word 'autonomy' at all. Thus, among Kant's formulations of the categorical imperative are these famous and stirring commands:

> Act only in accordance with a maxim through which you can at the same time will that it be a universal law. (4:421)

> Act so that you always treat humanity, in your own person as well as in the person of every other, at the same time as an end, never merely as a means. (4:429)

All maxims from one's own legislation should harmonize into a possible realm of ends, as with a realm of nature. (4:436)

An interpretation of the *Groundwork* must explain not only what these formulas mean, how they relate to each other, and how they relate to any normal conceptions of our moral obligations, but also how they relate to the conception of autonomy as the fundamental aim of human reason itself. The argument of this book will be that what Kant means by autonomy is nothing less than that condition in which human beings both individually and collectively can preserve and promote their freedom of choice and action to the greatest extent possible, that this is in his view the most fundamental value of human beings, and that adherence to the norms expressed by these formulas is in fact the means of realizing the goal of autonomy so understood. But the connection between the formulations of the categorical imperative and the goal of individual and collective human freedom is often beneath the surface of Kant's text.

This was not the case in many of Kant's other writings and statements in the period leading up to the *Groundwork*, however, so before turning to our main text we will take a brief look at some of these other sources. In these earlier texts, Kant suggests an argument like this: (1) freedom of choice and action is our most fundamental value; (2) but while any individual choice or action may be free considered by itself, freedom can be preserved over a multitude of actions of one or multiple individuals only if it is exercised in accordance with a law of self-consistency, that is, a rule that allows only those free acts that are maximally compatible with others; and (3) while the self-consistency of freedom provides, so to speak, the moral form of human action, the matter of action is the satisfaction of those particular desires of oneself and others that are compatible with this form – the sum of which satisfaction constitutes the greatest happiness that is compatible with the greatest virtue. In the *Groundwork*, these three claims are reflected by the three formulations of the categorical imperative cited in the previous paragraph: the premise (1) that freedom is our ultimate value lies behind the command always to treat humanity as an end and never merely as a means; the claim (2) that we should act only on maxims that can also be universal laws reflects the thesis that freedom can be preserved and promoted only if it is exercised in accordance with a requirement of the self-consistency of all free acts; and the claim (3) that the formal consistency of free acts is to be realized in the pursuit of particular human ends is reflected in Kant's conception of the realm of ends as 'a whole of all ends (of rational beings as ends in themselves as well as of the particular ends that each may set for himself)' (4:433). The present chapter will set out the evidence for this argument in the texts leading up to the *Groundwork*, while the remainder of the commentary will show how this argument can be found in the *Groundwork*. We will also see, however, that in his early writings Kant offered a psychological explanation of step (1), the premise that autonomy has absolute value, based on empirical claims about human nature. Kant rejects such a foundation for morality in the *Groundwork*, so we will have to ask whether he succeeds in providing an alternative foundation for this basic premise there.

The first two steps of Kant's argument are concisely expressed in a few pages of the lectures on ethics that Kant gave in the years leading up to the *Groundwork*. Kant based these lectures on the textbooks of Alexander Gottlieb Baumgarten (1714–62), a second-generation Wolffian, who divided all duties into duties toward God, duties toward oneself, and duties toward others. Kant dismissed the idea that we could have any duty toward God except that of fulfilling our duties toward ourselves and other human beings (thus rejecting the Lutheran doctrine that salvation is earned by faith alone rather than by works) and commenced his own catalogue of our real duties with our duties toward ourselves, the fulfillment of which he regarded as the necessary condition of fulfilling our duties toward others. He then asked 'On what then rests the principle of all duties toward oneself,' and answered,

> Freedom is on the one hand that capacity which gives all other capacities infinite usefulness, it is the highest degree of life, it is that property which is a necessary condition that underlies all perfections. All animals have the capacity to use their powers in accordance with their choice, but this choice is not free, but is rather necessitated through incentives and stimuli, in their actions there is *bruta necessitas*; if all beings had a power of choice so bound to sensory drives, the world would have no value; however, the inner value of the world, the *summum bonum*, is freedom in accordance with a power of choice that is not necessitated to act. Freedom is thus the inner value of the world. On the other hand, however, insofar as it is not restricted under a certain rule of its

conditioned use, it is the most terrible thing there can be . . . . If freedom is not restricted by means of objective rules, then the greatest wild disorder results, for it is uncertain whether humans would not use their powers to destroy themselves, others, and all of nature . . . What is the condition, under which freedom is [to be] restricted? This is the law. The universal law is thus: Conduct yourself so that in all actions regularity prevails . . . Freedom can be consistent with itself only under certain conditions, otherwise it collides with itself.[1]

Kant illustrates what he has in mind with a number of examples, the simplest of which is the duty to avoid drunkenness: the decision to get drunk may be a perfectly free decision considered by itself, but it can have the effect of destroying one's capacity for further free choices for the following hours, or for good if one is so unfortunate as to ram one's car into a tree while drunk. So drunkenness is not a condition in which freedom 'is in harmony with itself,' but one in which it may 'collide with itself.'[2] Kant does not explicitly add this, but one's free choice to get drunk might also collide with and undermine the freedom of others, as when the drunk driver crashes his car not into a tree but into the car of another, innocent family, incapacitating or killing them and thereby restricting or destroying their freedom of choice and action.

This passage illustrates the first two of Kant's central claims: that freedom has a fundamental value, but that the full value of freedom for each and for all can be realized only if each exercises his or her freedom in a way that is consistent with his or her further freedom as well as with the freedom of others affected by his or her choices and actions. But it does not touch upon Kant's third claim, that the form of the self-consistent exercise of freedom must be applied to the matter of particular human aims and goals, and thus that the lawful exercise of freedom should yield human happiness even though its value does not depend upon that result. And even the first two steps could use more explanation than Kant gives them here. However, various of Kant's own notes from the same years as these lectures do shed light on each of these three points, as do a set of lectures on political philosophy that Kant gave while he was writing the *Groundwork*.

Several notes clearly assert the fundamental value of freedom, that is, that freedom has an intrinsic value that is not dependent on its usefulness for some other end and an unconditional value that cannot be compromised by anything except its own self-destruction. As early as 1769–70, Kant wrote in his copy of Baumgarten's *Introduction to Practical Philosophy* that

> The understanding is only mediately good, as a means to another good or to happiness. The immediate good can be found only in freedom. . . . Hence nothing has an absolute worth but persons, and this consists in the goodness of their free power of choice. Just as freedom contains the first ground of everything that begins, so it is also that which alone contains self-consistent goodness.[3]

In 1776–8, Kant noted in his copy of Baumgarten's *Metaphysics* (the textbook for his metaphysics course), that 'Nothing is absolutely good (unconditioned in every respect) except the existence of freely acting beings.'[4] Around the same time, he wrote again in his copy of Baumgarten's *Introduction* that

> The dignity of human nature lies solely in freedom; through it we alone can become worthy of any good. But the dignity of a human being (worthiness) rests on the use of freedom, whereby he makes himself worthy of everything good. He makes himself worthy of this good, however, when he also works toward participating in it as much as lies in his natural talents and is allowed by outer agreement with the freedom of others.[5]

Here Kant adds a point that will not be central to the argument of the *Groundwork*, although it is central to the connection of moral virtue to happiness in the *Critique of Practical Reason* and further writings, namely that exercising one's freedom in a way consistent with the freedom of others makes one worthy of participating in the good outcome of the harmonious exercise of the freedom of all, although the value of freedom is intrinsic rather than dependent on this benefit. We will stick here to the point that freedom has an intrinsic value but that this value can only be realized if freedom is exercised in a rule-governed rather than unruly way. Kant also emphasized this point in the introductory lecture in his course on political philosophy ('natural right') in 1784 when he wrote that

If only rational beings can be ends in themselves, this cannot be because they have reason, but because they have freedom. Reason is merely a means. . . . Without reason a being cannot be an end in itself, for it cannot be conscious of its existence, nor reflect on it. But reason does not constitute the cause that the human being is an end in himself, that he has dignity that cannot be replaced by any equivalent. Reason does not give us that dignity. . . . Freedom, only freedom alone, makes it that we are ends in ourselves.[6]

This passage is important, because it shows that Kant does not value human beings strictly because of their *rationality*; his claim here is that our unconditional value lies in our capacity for freedom, but that reason has an instrumental value because it is by its means that we can figure out how to use our freedom self-consistently, that is, to make each use of our freedom compatible with its preservation and promotion in ourselves and others.

2. AUTONOMY AND RULES

None of these passages quite explains why we should believe that freedom has unconditional value, but let us leave that difficult question aside for a moment as we follow the thread of Kant's thought to his second step, already suggested in the last passage, that the role of rules is to make the use of freedom self-consistent, or to enable it to be preserved and promoted by our individual actions. This is a point that Kant repeatedly stresses in his notes. As early as 1764–8, Kant stated the reason why we need to apply reason and its rules to the exercise of our freedom: 'All right action is a *maximum* of the free power of choice when it is taken reciprocally.'[7] That is, our actions do not exist in isolation, but they affect each other, so in any particular situation we must choose an action that allows for the maximum of freedom for ourselves and others rather than any action which unnecessarily restricts that freedom – but we need reason in order to figure out which action that is. In 1776–8, he wrote:

The *principium* of **moral judgment** (the *principium* of the conformity of freedom with reason in general, i.e., lawfulness in accordance with universal conditions of consensus) is the rule for the subordination of freedom under the *principium* of the universal consensus of freedom with itself (with regard to oneself as well as other persons).[8]

This again suggests that reason must be used in order to determine how to make any particular free act consistent with the 'universal consensus of freedom with itself,' a consensus that preserves both one's own freedom and the freedom of others. Another note from the same period states that 'The primary ought is a condition under which alone freedom becomes a capacity in accordance with constant rules that determine *a priori*. . . . The will that is limited by no object and hence is pure must first not contradict itself, and freedom . . . must have unity.'[9]

In one key note, Kant adds that in order to preserve our freedom and that of others we need to act in accordance with rules because the only alternative is to be pushed around by our mere impulses, which, however, can readily conflict either with other of our own impulses or with those of others, which would leave either ourselves or others unfree to act as they might wish to on other occasions:

> Only it was necessary that our understanding at the same time projected universal rules, in accordance with which we had to order, restrict, and make coherent the efforts at our happiness, so that our blind impulses will not push us now here, now there, just by chance. Since the latter commonly conflict with one another, a judgment was necessary, which with regard to all of those impulses projects rules impartially, and thus in abstraction from all inclination, through the pure will alone, which rules, valid for all actions and for all human beings, would produce the greatest harmony of a human being with himself and with others.[10]

Only using our reason to provide rules for our actions can free us from being pushed around by impulses, whether our own or for that matter someone else's, which could contradict each other and undermine our freedom.

But what kind of rules could Kant have in mind, and what could he mean by rules that are 'valid for all actions and for all human beings' in 'abstraction from all inclination'? He cannot simply mean that we should act on rules that ignore all inclinations or impulses, or on the single rule that we should always ignore inclinations, for if none of us had any inclinations, there would be no need for any of us to act at all. Human actions are meant to satisfy human needs, which are revealed by desires, impulses, or inclinations. So what Kant has in mind can really be the rule to act only on those inclinations of oneself or others, action upon which is consistent with the continued freedom of oneself and others to act upon further inclinations that are also compatible with this condition – in other words, the rule to act only on inclinations toward ends that can be part of a realm of ends, 'of rational beings as ends in themselves as well as of the particular ends that each may set for himself.'

Kant makes this clear in several other striking notes. One crucial note says that

> Moral philosophy is the science of ends insofar as they are determined through pure reason. Or of the unity of all ends (that they do not conflict with themselves) of rational beings. The matter of the good is empirical, the form given *a priori*.[11]

Kant's use of the distinction between form and matter here suggests that the self-consistent exercise of freedom is a formal constraint on individual actions, but that those actions will themselves be in pursuit of empirically given ends, that is, ends suggested by naturally occurring desires and inclinations. So the demand of morality is not to abnegate all particular desires, but rather to pursue the satisfaction only of those that are consistent with the maximal intra- and interpersonal exercise of freedom. In another note, he says that 'Your actions ought to agree with your freedom and with what is universal in your inclinations, with the freedom of others and with what is universal in their inclinations.'[12] By 'universal' he cannot mean an inclination that one always has or that everyone has, but only an inclination the satisfaction of which is consistent with the universality of freedom, that is, the preservation and promotion of maximal freedom for oneself and others.

If what morality requires is not that we simply abnegate all inclinations, but rather act only on those that are consistent with the maximum of freedom for ourselves and others, then morality does not sever all connection with happiness, for happiness consists in the satisfaction of inclinations. Morality therefore actually tells us to pursue happiness, but only under certain constraints. Kant will stress in the *Groundwork* that the desire for happiness can never be an adequate or estimable *motivation* for the conduct demanded by morality, but as he does that we will have to keep in mind that morality is actually the form that governs the pursuit of happiness. This is a point that in the *Groundwork* Kant makes only implicitly through his concept of the realm of ends.

3. THE VALUE OF AUTONOMY

We have seen how the three steps of the argument outlined at the beginning of this chapter are suggested by Kant's pre-*Groundwork* texts. Let us now return to the difficult question of why we should believe that maximal freedom for ourselves and others is in fact the fundamental value that is to be fostered by the adherence to moral laws. Kant actually suggests several different approaches to this problem.

In the lectures on natural right, Kant suggests an argument that not everything can have merely instrumental value, but there must be something of unconditional value if there is not to be an infinite regress of values – just as in metaphysics (we might think) there must be something that is self-caused in order to avoid an infinite regress of causes: 'That something must exist as an end in itself, and that not everything can exist merely as a means, is just as necessary in the system of ends as the existence of an *ens a se* is in the series of efficient causes.'[13] This seems to be the premise for an argument that because all sorts of other things can be used as means for the purposes freely chosen by the human will, and in that way have instrumental value as means for human ends, the freedom of the human will itself must be the end for which those things are the means, or have an unconditional value that is the basis for their conditional value. 'What can be considered merely as a means has value as a means only when it is used. For that there must be a thing that is an end in itself.'[14] However, although there are some interpreters who find such an argument at the heart of the *Groundwork*, there are two problems with it. First, Kant argues extensively in the *Critique of Pure Reason* that our tendency to posit something unconditioned at the beginning of every series, for example a first cause at the beginning of the series of all events, can never be confirmed by our experience, and so yields no actual cognition, but only a 'regulative' ideal to guide our further inquiry; so likewise there is no sufficient ground to assume that there is necessarily something of unconditional value at the basis of all instrumental value in the practical sphere either, but this might at best be only another regulative ideal. Second, the precise wording of Kant's argument in the lectures on natural right suggests that he appeals to the unconditional value of the human will to explain the instrumental value of other things that humans can use only because he thinks that the human will *is* an end in itself: 'If there were no end, then the means would also be in vain and have no value. – The human is an end, thus it is contradictory that he should merely be a means.'[15] That is, the unconditional value of the freedom of the human will can stop an infinite regress of merely instrumental values only because it is an independent fact that it is an end in itself – but that fact still needs to be explained.

That leaves two other approaches. In one striking note, Kant suggests a psychological approach to our problem:

> Everything finally comes down to life; that which animates, or the feeling of the promotion of life, is agreeable. Life is unity; hence all taste has as its *principio* the unity of animating suggestions.
>
> Freedom is the original life and, in its coherence, the condition of the correspondence of all life; hence that which promotes the feeling of universal life, or the feeling of the promotion of universal life, produces a pleasure.[16]

This thought stems from a psychology according to which our greatest source of pleasure is free activity; the idea is then that such pleasure is maximized by maximizing the scope for free activity, and paradoxical as it may sound, doing this depends upon subjecting our freedom to a rule, namely the rule that says we should always exercise our freedom in a way that is consistent with the maximal scope for our freedom on other occasions. Only in that way will we actually be able to enjoy a maximum of activity, life, or animation.

Now it might seem as if such an argument could generate at most the rule that one should always act in a way that maximizes the scope of one's *own* continued freedom; why should the freedom of others contribute to the maximization of my own feeling of life? This problem could be avoided if it could be shown that maximizing one's own freedom in fact requires preserving or even promoting the freedom of others, so that they will reciprocate by not restricting and even promoting one's own freedom. It might be possible to make such an argument. But even if that can be done, the present approach still seems to depend on one or more claims about human psychology that are contingent, if they are facts at all, namely the claims that everyone enjoys the exercise of their own freedom and that people whose own freedom is respected and promoted will reciprocate by respecting and promoting the freedom of others. Because these are at best contingent facts about human beings, Kant does not employ this approach to the value of freedom in the *Groundwork*. And although he does recognize a psychological love of freedom as late as his textbook on anthropology, there he also warns that it can actually become an irrational passion or mania[17] – so a psychological desire for freedom seems like something that needs to be controlled by reason, but not something that is of itself of unconditional value.

So although Kant suggests both a metaphysical and a psychological approach to explaining the unconditional value of human freedom, each of these seems problematic by his own lights. The remaining possibility is a purely normative approach, one on which the fundamental value of freedom is somehow shown to underlie all our other norms without being derivable from any non-normative metaphysical or empirical fact. Kant suggests such an approach both early and late in his career, but also suggests that a fundamental norm is 'indemonstrable' – what it means for it to be fundamental is precisely that it cannot be derived from anything else, and therefore cannot be explained. Thus, in his early essay on the principles of natural theology and morality, he wrote that the formal rules to seek perfection and avoid imperfection can only be applied in conjunction with certain 'indemonstrable material principles of practical cognition,'[18] and in the *Critique of Practical Reason*, he will argue that we can infer the actuality of our freedom from our recognition of our obligation under the moral law but that we cannot deduce the latter from anything else – it is again indemonstrable. In the notes leading up to the *Groundwork*, however, he may suggest a slightly different approach, namely that we all recognize a dignity in not being pushed around by our emotions and impulses but in instead making our own choices about whether or not to act on the former. In one note, he says that 'Personality is the independence of the will from inclinations,' and that 'morality is correspondence with personality.'[19] Another says that 'The human being as a being that has understanding must be very dissatisfying in his own eyes if his understanding is subject to the inclinations and does not stand under a rule with regard to his end.'[20] And another says 'Freedom has dignity on account of its independence.'[21] Such comments suggest that we all feel that there is something undignified and contemptible in being dominated by our own impulses (including the impulse to be dominated by the impulses of others), and something noble and praiseworthy in subjecting our impulses to the rule of reason in order to preserve our freedom. Saying that freedom has unconditional value, contrasted to the conditional value of gratifying any particular inclination, is at least a way of formalizing this feeling if not of explaining it.

A similar thought about dignity and worth comes up in some of Kant's comments about happiness. Thus he says that 'The *principium* of morals is autocracy of freedom with regard to all happiness or the epigenesis of happiness in accordance with universal laws of freedom.'[22] Sometimes it seems as if what Kant means by this is the Stoic doctrine that our happiness is more *secure* if we place it in the realization only of ends that are within our own control.[23] But more often what he seems to mean is that we find nothing *admirable* in happiness insofar as it is the product of mere luck, but do approve of it when it is the product of our own free choices and efforts. Thus 'Happiness has no self-sufficient worth insofar as it is a gift of nature or luck. Its origin from freedom is what constitutes its self-sufficiency and harmony.'[24] Even when it comes to happiness, we can distinguish between mere pleasure and our satisfaction in being the author of our own condition – in other words, what originates in freedom has a kind of dignity that would not attach to it otherwise. Again, we can put this by saying that freedom has an unconditional value in contrast to the merely conditional value of anything else.

In this chapter, it has been suggested that three of Kant's most striking formulations of the categorical imperative in the *Groundwork* can be associated with his earlier statements of the argument that freedom has unconditional value, that a rule of its self-consistency is necessary in order to realize and maximize freedom, yet that this rule is also only the form for our action, the matter of which is the pursuit of particular ends, so that the pursuit of freedom should in fact also lead to happiness. Our task now is to locate this argument beneath the dense surface of the *Groundwork*, as well as to see if that work has something more to say about the first premise of this whole argument, namely the claim that the maximization of freedom has unconditional value. In particular, since in the *Groundwork* Kant explicitly denies that moral philosophy can be grounded on any merely empirical facts about human nature, we must ask whether Kant there offers a genuine alternative to the psychological argument for the value of autonomy in his earlier writings.

Study Questions

1. Is it really a fact about human psychology that all humans value freedom more than the results of any particular use of freedom?
2. Can freedom really be preserved only through the use of rules?
3. Can psychology explain why one person should value the freedom of others?

CHAPTER 3

READING THE TEXT: PREFACE

1. THE PURITY OF MORAL PHILOSOPHY

Kant's Preface to the *Groundwork* seems to be concerned largely with housekeeping, that is, with explaining how moral philosophy fits into Kant's larger system, and to say almost nothing about the distinctive contents of the moral philosophy to be offered in the work. But the methodological points that Kant discusses are in fact intimately connected to the content of his moral philosophy, so we must not ignore what might seem like mere technicalities.

Kant begins the Preface by distinguishing logic from metaphysics, and within metaphysics the metaphysics of nature from the metaphysics of morals. Logic 'concerns itself merely with the form of the understanding and reason itself and the universal rules of thinking in general, without distinction among objects' (*G*, 4:387). Metaphysics, by contrast, is a form of 'material cognition,' that is, it does concern itself with particular kinds of 'determinate objects and the laws to which they are subject.' In Kant's view there are two main branches of metaphysics because there are two main kinds of objects and laws: there are natural objects and the 'laws in accordance with which everything happens,' and there are free actions and the laws that apply to them, namely the laws 'in accordance with which everything ought to happen' (4:387–8). The former are the subject-matter of 'physics' or the science of nature; the latter are the subject-matter of 'ethics' or the doctrine of morals. Next, Kant divides both the physics and morals into a 'rational' and an 'empirical' part: the former is supposed to 'develop its doctrines strictly *a priori*,' and can thus be called '**pure** philosophy,' while the latter is 'grounded on experience' and is '**empirical**' (4:388). Thus physics has both an 'empirical but also a rational part,' and morals too is to be divided into two parts, one of which concerns only its purely rational principles and is to be called morals proper, while the other concerns the application of those principles to the actual conditions of human existence, and 'could be called **practical anthropology.**' The *Groundwork for the Metaphysics of Morals* is supposed to concern itself strictly with the purely rational principles of morality, while the specific duties of human beings that can be derived from the application of these rational principles to some basic empirical facts about the human condition are to be presented in a subsequent work of 'practical anthropology,' the *Metaphysics of Morals* that Kant finally published in 1797.

All of this may seem like a dry matter of definitions, but there are several points here that call for comment. First, the way Kant uses the terms 'ethics' (*Sitten*) and 'morals' (*Moral*, sometimes *Moralität*) can cause confusion. In English, 'ethics' and 'morals' or 'morality' can be used interchangeably, and Kant's initial use of 'ethics' suggests that this is the case for him too. In German, the word *Sitten* could also be used in the general sense of 'customs,' as a translation for the Greek word *ethos* or the Latin word *mores*, without a strongly normative connotation. Kant does not use the word in this sense. As he continues, however, it also becomes clear that he does not generally use 'ethics' and 'morals' interchangeably. As we have already seen, he says that the term 'morals' is properly used to designate only the purely rational part of his theory of behavioral norms; and in his later work the term 'ethics' is actually used quite restrictively, to mean not even the whole of practical anthropology or the theory of our particular duties, but only a part of that, namely those of our duties that cannot be coercively enforced by means of a legal and penal system. Those duties that can be so enforced are the subject-matter of 'right,' or are 'juridical duties,' while the non-coercively enforceable, 'ethical' duties are also called duties of 'virtue' and the later work is correspondingly divided into a 'doctrine of right' and a 'doctrine of 'virtue.' This leaves no general term for the sum of our particular duties of both right and virtue except for 'practical anthropology,' which, however, Kant does not subsequently use. And it leaves both books, the *Grundlegung zur Metaphysik der Sitten* and the *Metaphysik der Sitten*, misleadingly titled: their titles suggest that they concern the principles and contents of our non-coercively enforceable, 'ethical' duties only, when it is clear that they concern

the principles and contents of all of our duties, a fact reflected by
the use of the more general term 'morals' to translate *Sitten* in the
standard English translations of the titles of these works as the
Groundwork for the Metaphysics of Morals and the *Metaphysics of
Morals* respectively.

The second point to notice is that Kant's definitions already imply
a profound substantive point, for by separating the doctrine of
morals from the doctrine of nature instead of treating it as a part
of the latter, Kant implies that moral principles and the possibility
of conduct in accordance with them cannot be treated naturalisti-
cally. In Kant's view, moral principles must have a source in a human
faculty that is not explicable by any merely natural laws, and the possibility of conduct in accordance with moral principles must presuppose the freedom of the human will from determination by the
laws of nature. In other words, by means of his contrast between
physics and morals, Kant clearly intends to contrast his approach to
moral philosophy from that of the Scottish school of Hutcheson
and Hume and of sympathetic spirits among the French *philosophes*
such as Denis Diderot, who sought naturalistic – what we would now
call 'evolutionary' – explanations of human moral sensibilities and
dispositions. Of course, Kant's approach places a heavy burden of
proof on him: he will owe us not only a plausible account of how
there can be a non-natural source for moral principles and moral
conduct and how we can know about it, but also an account of how
this non-natural element in human nature relates to the naturalistic
aspect, which can be explained according to naturalistic laws of
human physiology and psychology. This is a central issue for Kant
in all of his writings in moral philosophy.

Finally, we must ask what Kant means by referring to the purely
rational and *a priori* part of moral philosophy. We can break this
down into two questions: what he means by saying that the fundamental principles of morality must be pure and *a priori*, and what he
means by claiming that they are rational, or have their source in our
(in some sense not merely natural) faculty of reason. The first of
these questions is the easier of the two. In the *Critique of Pure
Reason*, Kant explains that any principle that is known to be universally and necessarily true must be known *a priori*, that is, prior to
any particular experience – prior not in a temporal sense, since from
a chronological point of view 'all our cognition begins with experience' (*PureR*, B 1), but in a justificatory sense. Universal and

necessary truth cannot be known from experience of any particular examples, since, as Hume had pointed out so effectively in his famous argument about the rationality of our belief in causation, any finite number of experiences proves only that some fact is true in those cases, not in any unexperienced cases.[1] In Kant's words, 'Experience never gives its judgments true or strict but only assumed and comparative **universality** . . . Thus if a judgment is thought in strict universality, i.e., in such a way that no exception at all is allowed to be possible, then it is not derived from experience, but is rather valid absolutely *a priori*' (B 3–4). So Kant means that fundamental moral laws cannot be derived from empirical study of actual examples of human conduct – not merely because, as he will later observe, it is so hard to determine in practice whether any actual human being ever is or has been fully motivated by morality alone (*G*, 4:406), but because as a matter of logic no finite number of even conclusive examples of morally appropriate human conduct could yield any truly universal and necessary moral laws. Of course, all of this is negative, telling us what the sources of *a priori* knowledge *cannot* be; it takes much of the rest of the *Critique of Pure Reason* to explain what the sources of *a priori* knowledge in the metaphysics of nature are, and it will likewise be a central issue for Kant's moral philosophy to explain what the sources of an *a priori* principle of morality are, specifically that human reason itself provides a truly universal and necessary moral law that no amount of experience can generate.

So we need to turn next to Kant's conception of reason as a source of *a priori* moral law. But before we do that, we should ask what makes Kant so confident that there is such a thing as *a priori* moral law? In his theoretical philosophy, Kant held that in spite of Hume's doubts about causation we can be sure that there is *a priori* knowledge of universal and necessary truths from the case of mathematics and natural science (*PureR*, B 14–18), and then he argued that the only possible explanation of that *a priori* knowledge reveals that we have *a priori* knowledge of the general principle that every event has a cause. In moral philosophy, Kant holds that the possibility of a 'pure moral philosophy . . . cleansed of everything that might be merely empirical and that belongs to anthropology' is 'evident of itself from the common idea of duty and moral law' (*G*, 4:389). In other words, Kant takes it that everyone assumes that there are universal and necessary moral principles, and that the task for moral philosophy is not to prove that this is so but rather just to identify the fundamental moral law and explain the possibility of our knowledge of it. His project is not so much to refute someone who is already skeptical about the existence of universal and necessary moral laws as rather to prevent such skepticism from arising by showing that the common assumption that there are such laws is indeed well-founded.

2. THE RATIONALITY OF MORALITY

Let us now return to the question of what Kant means by reason and thus what he could have in mind in arguing that the fundamental principle of morality can be known to be universally and necessarily true because it originates from reason itself. Kant divides the human cognitive powers into the 'lower' power of sensibility and the 'higher' power of intellect, which is in turn divided into understanding, reason, and (sometimes) judgment. For Kant, sensibility is the power to have immediate, singular representations of particular objects, or 'intuitions,' whether these are abstract mathematical objects that we encounter in 'pure intuition' or concrete objects that we encounter in 'empirical intuition' by means of our ordinary senses such as sight and touch (*PureR*, A 19–21/B 33–5 and A 320/B 376–7).[2] Understanding is the ability to formulate concepts, which are general representations of types of objects by means of predicates that can be shared by many individuals, whether these are *a priori* concepts or 'categories' such as 'substance' and 'causation' or empirical concepts such as 'cat' or 'collision.' Sometimes Kant assigns the ability to apply concepts to actual objects to the faculty of understanding, and sometimes he assigns this ability to a separate faculty of judgment. Finally, Kant introduces the faculty of reason, but assigns several functions to it. One function of reason, its 'logical' function, is simply to perform inferences on judgments supplied to it by other faculties. Thus, understanding might supply the judgments 'All humans are mortal' and 'Socrates is a human,' but it would be reason that draws the conclusion 'Therefore Socrates is mortal.' But Kant also assigns to reason the ability to form 'transcendental ideas' of the 'unconditioned,' or of things that are grounds or explanations for other things but require no ground or explanation themselves: ideas such as God as the uncaused cause, the soul as the subject or all experiences, or freedom as the ability to initiate actions and therefore chains of events without itself being dependent upon any antecedent cause. Kant attempts to link these two aspects of reason by arguing that reason forms its ideas of the unconditioned in order to put an end to infinite regresses of inferences,[3] but that step of his theory need not concern us here; we can work merely with Kant's idea of reason as the source of ideas of the unconditioned, and then ask how this will be the source of a fundamental principle of morality that is universally and necessarily true and thus can and must be known to be valid *a priori*.

Kant's basic idea must be that the fundamental principle of morality must come from reason because even the common ideas of duty or moral laws recognize that moral law is unconditional, that is, it applies to one regardless of whatever particular desires one might have, thus regardless of whether in some ordinary sense one wants to behave as morality dictates or would prefer to behave otherwise. But how is this to be linked to Kant's special idea of the unconditioned? Kant certainly does not spell this out in the Preface to the *Groundwork*, but what we will see as we interpret the main text is that his underlying idea is that the moral law must come from reason because it is the law that is necessary in order to preserve human freedom whole and unimpaired, and also the law that is necessary in order to allow particular human intentions and goals to be integrated into a whole in which as many as possible are included. In other words, Kant's ideas of individual maxims that could also serve as universal laws, of a recognition of each and every human being as an end in itself, and of a kingdom of ends in which all are treated as ends in themselves and their particular ends are also honored as far as is possible for all, are all products of pure reason, ideas that apply the general idea of the unconditioned to various aspects of free human conduct.

Another point that must be considered before we leave Kant's concept of reason is his insistence that if a law is to be universally valid then it 'must not be valid merely for human beings, as if other rational beings did not have to heed it,' and thus that 'the ground of obligation must not be sought in the nature of the human being or in the circumstances of the world in which he is placed, but strictly *a priori* in concepts of pure reason' (*G*, 4:389). There are two points to be made here. First, Kant is not committed to the actual existence of any rational beings other than human beings, such as angels or God, and does not seek moral laws valid for all rational beings because he believes that there are rational beings other than human beings. His insistence that moral laws must be valid for all possible rational beings is a way of saying that moral laws must be valid for all human beings regardless of any particular features of human psychology, thus independently of any particular desires or inclinations, and that this can be so only if moral laws are grounded in reason alone, a capability that could be shared with beings whose psychology might otherwise be very different from our own. But, second, Kant's insistence that the *derivation* of moral laws must be 'cleansed' of everything empirical and valid for any possible rational being does not mean that the *application* of moral laws cannot take into account specific features of human nature. On the contrary, Kant's suggestion that the application of moral laws is the subject of 'practical anthropology' means that the derivation of particular duties from the general principles of morality does and must take account of certain basic facts about human physiology, psychology, and circumstances. For example, Kant's derivation of the duty to avoid drunkenness and gluttony in the *Metaphysics of Morals* depends on the fact that excessive amounts of alcohol and food impair people's ability to exercise their freedom rationally, even though we could imagine other rational beings with a different constitution for whom this is not true, who would therefore be morally free to drink and eat as much as they like; and his derivation of the right to private property depends on the fact that human beings need physical locations in order to rest and grow food or do other work, even though again this might not be true for other sorts of rational beings. So in Kant's moral philosophy the fundamental principle of morality must be valid for any and rational beings, but the specific duties that this principle implies for human beings will be valid only for human beings.

3.   THE NEED FOR MORAL PHILOSOPHY

But now let us ask a different question. If Kant is so sure that the 'common idea of duty and moral laws' makes it self-evident that there are *a priori* moral laws, why do we need moral philosophy at all? Kant makes two statements that bear on this question. First, he says that

A metaphysics of morals is indispensably necessary, not merely in order to investigate the sources of the practical principles lying in our reason *a priori*, but rather because morals themselves remain subject to all sorts of corruption as long as that guideline and supreme norm for their correct judgment is lacking. For in the case of that which is to be morally good, it is not enough that it is **in accordance** with the moral law, but it must also happen **for its sake**; otherwise that accordance is only very contingent and precarious, because the non-moral ground may, to be sure, produce actions that are in accord with the law now and then, but will often produce actions that are opposed to the law. (*G*, 4:389–90)

And subsequently he says that 'The present groundwork is nothing more than the search for and establishment of **the supreme principle of morality**' (4:392). These comments intimate several points that will become clearer as Kant's argument develops. The key is Kant's suggestion that common sense in some way contains the fundamental principle of morality but is also readily liable to corruption, a danger that only moral philosophy can avert. There are several things he has in mind here. First, common sense may recognize the moral principle in some form, but unless the principle is formulated as clearly as only philosophy can do, there is the danger that it can be misunderstood and therefore misapplied, leading to actions that may seem morally appropriate but are not. Second, moral philosophy is needed to show that the fundamental principle of morality is not only the *norm* or *criterion* of right actions but also the only adequate *motivation* for them, because any other motivation, for example thinking that one's interest in one's own long-term happiness is best served merely by outwardly appearing always to act as morality requires, cannot be counted upon to yield morally appropriate action in every circumstance – if one acts in accordance with morality only in order to enjoy the good will of others, one will have no motive to act morally when one thinks no one else will find out what one has done. Finally, even the best-intentioned people, for whom the thought of the moral law is a completely sufficient motivation, could lose their commitment always to do what morality demands, even when that is hard or painful, unless they are sure that to do so is really within their power, that is, to use the language of the *Critique of Practical Reason* and the *Religion*,[4] unless they are sure that they *can* do what they know they *ought* to do. In other words, maintaining our commitment to morality may require a proof that we have freedom of the will, and so can always choose to do what morality demands no matter what our prior history might suggest we could be expected to choose, a proof which only philosophy can provide.

As Kant puts it at the end of the first section of the *Groundwork*, we need moral philosophy in order to protect 'innocence' – our natural awareness of what morality demands and our natural tendency to want to do it – from an equally **natural dialectic**, that is, a propensity to quibble against those strict laws of duty and to draw into doubt their validity, or at least their purity and strictness and, where possible, to make them more suited to our wishes and inclinations, i.e., to corrupt them at bottom and to destroy their entire dignity' (4:405). In order to resolve this 'natural dialectic' and address the concerns we considered in the previous paragraph, two main issues will have to be addressed: first, the principle of morality will have to be distinguished from any principle that makes happiness, one's own or even that of others, the primary goal of morality and the desire for happiness the motivation for morality, and second, the existence of the free will that makes it possible for us to do as morality commands and thus prevents our motivation to do that from being undermined will have to be demonstrated. The first of these tasks, that is, distinguishing both the principle of and the motivation for morality from a concern for happiness, will be a primary concern of the second section of the *Groundwork*, while the third section will be devoted to 'establishing' the principle of morality but also in the course of so doing demonstrating that it is always possible for us to do what morality commands.

4. THE METHOD OF MORAL PHILOSOPHY

We will conclude this chapter by considering two comments about his method in the *Groundwork* that Kant makes in bringing his Preface to a close. In the first of these passages, Kant says that although there can be no other foundation for a groundwork for the metaphysics of morals than a 'critique of a **pure practical reason**,' such a critique is not as urgent as the critique of pure theoretical reason was, because while the latter was 'entirely dialectical,' that is, it gave rise to a tissue of metaphysical illusions that had to be completely unraveled, 'human reason in its moral application, even by the commonest understanding, can easily be brought to great correctness and completeness.' He also says that for a critique of pure practical reason to

31

be completed, 'its unity with speculative reason in a common princi-ple would have to be exhibited, because in the end it can only be one and the same reason, which must differ merely in its application,' but that to show that would require considerations that might be con-fusing to the reader (4:391). In other words, Kant suggests that while the pure use of theoretical reason leads to nothing but confusions that must be thoroughly criticized, moral philosophy has a core of common sense on which it can build, and even though, as we have just seen, common sense is subject to a 'natural dialectic,' somehow this can be resolved without such a thorough critique as was neces-sary in the case of theoretical reason and its dialectic. Or so at least Kant thought at the time he wrote the *Groundwork*. The fact that only three years later he published a *Critique of Practical Reason* instead of proceeding directly to the *Metaphysics of Morals* suggests that he may have rethought this view and concluded that the dialectical danger in practical reason is just as great as it is in the case of theor-etical reason, thus that a critique of pure practical is just as necessary as one of theoretical reason. A thorough exploration of that issue would be beyond the limits of the present book, however; we will have to confine ourselves to considering to what extent Kant bases the argument of the *Groundwork* on common moral sense and sensi-bilities, and to what extent he goes beyond this in appealing to more philosophical considerations to ground his argument.

Finally, Kant says that the method he will use in the *Groundwork* is one that 'proceeds analytically from common cognition [of moral-ity] to the determination of the supreme principle thereof and then in turn back synthetically from the examination of this principle and its sources to common cognition, in which its use is encountered,' and that this method leads to the division of the *Groundwork* into these three sections:

1. **First section.** Transition from the common rational cognition of morals to the philosophical.
2. **Second section.** Transition from popular moral philosophy to the metaphysics of morals.
3. **Third section.** Final step from the metaphysics of morals to the critique of pure practical reason. (4:392)

These claims need to be unpacked. First, we need to understand what Kant means by saying that the *Groundwork* will employ both

analytical and synthetical *methods*. This contrast has to be distinguished from the contrast between analytic and synthetic *judgments*
that Kant makes in the *Critique of Pure Reason*. That is the distinction between judgments in which the predicate-concept may clarify
but does not add anything to what is already contained in the
subject-concept, and which thus can be known to be true by the
application of logical analysis to the subject-concept alone, and
judgments in which the predicate-concept does make a genuine addition to the subject-concept and which thus, however they are to be
known, cannot be known on the basis of logic alone (*PureR*, A
6–10/B 10–14). Kant will in fact claim that the categorical imperative
is a synthetic *a priori* proposition that does add something to the
concept of a purely rational being, but that is not what he is talking
about here. Rather, here he is using a more traditional distinction
between regressive and progressive methods of *argument*, and claiming that he will use both in the course of the *Groundwork*. An analytical or regressive argument was traditionally one that infers back
from something taken to be a fact to its presuppositions or the conditions of its possibility, while a synthetic or progressive argument
was one that goes from some premise to its consequences. In this
sense, the first section of the *Groundwork*, which goes from some
common ideas about good will and duty to a philosophical formulation of the categorical imperative, would be analytical, for it infers
back from some common beliefs and practices to the principle on
which the former rest, while those parts of the second section in
which Kant provides some examples of commonly recognized duties
that can be inferred from his formulations of the categorical imperative could be considered synthetic, for they go from the principle
to its consequences. (Here the fact that the consequences are
commonly recognized duties also provides confirmation of the
correctness of Kant's analysis of the underlying principle.) In the
Prolegomena to Any Future Metaphysics, however, Kant departs
from the traditional distinction. He says that an analytical argument
or inquiry relies 'on something already known to be dependable,
from which we can . . . ascend to [its] sources,' which is in conformity
with the tradition, but introduces a new account of a synthetical
method when he says that such a method inquires 'within pure
reason itself, and seek[s] to determine within this source both the elements and the laws of its pure use, according to principles.'[5] This
suggests a different distribution of analytical and synthetical

moments in the *Groundwork*: the derivation of the fundamental principle of morality from common-sense ideas and practices in the first section remains analytical, but the derivation of the several formulations of the categorical from basic philosophical concepts in the second section will fit better with Kant's present definition of synthetical method, as will the establishment or proof of the validity of the moral law as well as the proof of the freedom of the will that are to be offered in the third section, both of which derive the consequences from certain philosophical assumptions about the nature of reason. In order to understand the complex structure of Kant's overall argument, we will therefore have to keep in mind both the traditional meaning of the distinction between analytical and synthetical methods and Kant's revised version of that distinction.

Finally, what does Kant mean by the 'transitions' in his titles for the three sections of the *Groundwork*? It would be easy to assume that he means the same thing in each case, something like 'leads to,' and also that he means to describe a continuous transition, in which the first section leads directly to the second and the second to the third. On this understanding, his titles would suggest that in the first section 'common rational cognition of morals' is supposed to lead to some key philosophical conclusions, that in the second section those key philosophical conclusions in turn lead to a more fully developed metaphysics of morals, including an enumeration of actual duties, and that in the third section that metaphysics of morals in turns leads to a critique of pure practical reason (though not, as Kant previously said, a *complete* critique). Such an understanding, however, would be misleading. The actual structure of Kant's argument is more like this: In the first section of the *Groundwork*, he will indeed show that common-sense moral ideas lead to a philosophically accurate – although not, as it turns out, complete – formulation of the categorical imperative. In the second section, however, he does not simply show that this result leads to a full metaphysics of morals. Rather, he argues first that 'popular moral philosophy,' based on empirical observation of the actual conduct of human beings and thus on the assumption that the proper principle of human action is based on the desire for happiness, has to *give way* to the purer formulation of the moral law that was derived from common sense. But then he also argues, although not explicitly, that this purer formulation has to make a 'transition' to 'metaphysics of morals' in two different senses. On the one hand, the formulations of the categorical imperative that are reached in the second section have to be shown to give rise to an adequate if also only general catalogue of our actual duties, which is what Kant means by a 'metaphysics of morals' in the later work of that title. But on the other hand, the several formulations of the categorical imperative have to be shown to be *grounded* in some fundamental philosophical conceptions of human reason, will, and value, which is closer to what Kant means by the phrase 'metaphysics of morals' in the Preface (e.g., 4:388–9). Finally, in the third section the 'metaphysics of morals' in this second sense, that is, the assumptions about human reason and will that ground the categorical imperative, will in turn have to be grounded in some even further and deeper philosophical investigations that merit the title of a 'critique of pure practical reason' – even though, as Kant has warned us, this critique will not be complete.

All of this will be a lot to keep in mind as we now begin our examination of the three main sections of the *Groundwork*. It will have been noticed, however, that in the Preface Kant has said nothing about the argument suggested in his preparatory notes and lectures, namely that it is the unconditional value of freedom of choice and action that grounds the categorical imperative, for it is only by adherence to the moral law that freedom can be preserved and promoted both in oneself and others. Our task in what follows will thus not only be that of seeing how the various tactics suggested by the Preface play out in the main text of the work, but also whether and if so how Kant's text implements the underlying strategy he previously suggested.

Study Questions
1. What is the difference between moral philosophy and ethics?
2. Why should moral philosophy be 'pure'?
3. What must reason be like if it is to be the source of pure moral philosophy?
4. Should moral philosophy use a single method, or should it, as Kant suggests, use multiple methods?

CHAPTER 4

READING THE TEXT: SECTION I.
FROM THE GOOD WILL TO
THE FORMULA OF UNIVERSAL LAW

1. INTRODUCTION

Section I of the *Groundwork* is to make a transition from 'common' to philosophical knowledge of morality. Specifically, the section examines what are supposed to be common-sense ideas about good will, the function of human reason, and duty, and from these derives a first statement of the fundamental principle of morality. Our task for this chapter is to consider Kant's interpretations of these common-sense ideas, to see whether they lead to the conception of the fundamental principle of morality that he claims they do, and to see how if at all his moves in the first section relate to the pre-*Groundwork* argument expounded in Chapter 2.

2. THE GOOD WILL

Kant begins Section I with the famous statement that 'There is nothing that it is possible to think of anywhere in the world, indeed even outside it, that can be held to be good without restriction except a **good will**' (4:393). This is supposed to be common sense, and Kant defends it by means of considerations that are also supposed to be acknowledged by common sense. He claims that '**talents** of the mind' such as 'understanding, wit, and judgment' and 'qualities of **temperament**' such as 'courage, resolution, and persistence' are no doubt often good but can also be 'extremely evil and deleterious' if the will and character that employs them is not good. He claims that '**gifts of fortune**' such as 'power, wealth, honor, even health, and the complete well-being and satisfaction with one's condition that goes under the name of **happiness**' are likewise often good, but can lead to arrogance (and no doubt bad consequences of that arrogance) if they are not governed by a good will. He also claims that a 'rational impartial observer' will not approve of the possession of these goods of fortune, including happiness, by someone who is 'adorned with no trace of a pure and good will.' Even qualities of character that are often 'advantageous to this good will and can facilitate its work,' such as 'moderation in affects and passions, self-control, and sober reflection,' are 'good in many contexts and even seem to constitute a part of the **inner** worth of a person' but still do not possess an 'inner unconditional worth'; their value instead 'still always presupposes a good will' (4:393–4). From the fact that none of these things, even happiness itself, possesses value except on the condition that it is accompanied by a good will, Kant infers that the good will itself must have unconditional value.

This is not a valid inference, for perhaps *nothing* possesses unconditional value, in which case we could not infer from the fact that none of these things possesses unconditional value that a good will does. Ultimately, Kant will have to provide a positive reason why we should think that a good will has unconditional value. That is a large challenge for the *Groundwork* as a whole. Further, Kant's initial move is one that almost any moral theory can make, and so does not by itself imply a particular conception of the moral principle in accordance with which a good will must act. *Almost* any moral theory, to be sure, for Kant's opening sally is effective at least against one tendency in ancient moral philosophy. Ancient moral philosophers such as the Stoics certainly agreed that gifts of fortune such as power and wealth were desirable but not morally valuable or 'choiceworthy.' But even the Stoics along with other ancient philosophers held that wisdom, courage, and prudence – in Kant's terminology, understanding, wit, and judgment; courage, resolution, and persistence; and moderation in affects and passions, self-control, and sober reflection – are, along with justice, cardinal virtues, and thus always intrinsically and unconditionally valuable. Kant is rejecting this claim, implying that these qualities are not really virtues at all unless they are governed by a good will (for which justice might have been the ancient category). But leaving aside this criticism of ancient moral philosophy, Kant's point could still be accommodated by most moral philosophies as long as they hold that when it comes to the moral evaluation of individuals' actions or characters, what counts is *what they intended* rather than *what they actually produced,* that is, the quality of their will rather than the quality of an outcome. For example, even a utilitarian who believes that what is good is simply whatever contributes to the greatest happiness for the greatest number could hold that individuals are morally good as long as they sincerely and fully *intend* and *try* to produce the greatest good for the greatest number, even if for reasons beyond their control their actions do not have that effect – in other words, as long as they act with a good will, as defined by the utilitarian.

Kant may have meant to avert this objection by including happiness itself along with intelligence, courage, and prudence on his list of things that are valuable only if they are accompanied by a good will. When he states that 'The good will is not good because of what it effects or accomplishes, not because of its usefulness for the attainment of any intended end, but only through the willing, i.e., in itself, and is to be esteemed incomparably higher than what could be brought about through it in behalf of any inclination or even, if one will, the sum of all inclinations' (4:394), he maintains that the good will is not good even because of an *intended outcome*. In other words, whereas other moralities may base their evaluations of action and character on *intended* rather than *actual outcomes*, Kant claims that moral value has nothing to do with the outcomes of actions at all, not even with intended outcomes. But in order to sustain this position, he is going to have to do more than appeal to the common intuition that in moral evaluation it is the quality of an individual's intention rather than the actual outcome of that intention that counts.

In fact, Kant presses his attack against utilitarianism – already prominent, before Jeremy Bentham, in the writings of Francis Hutcheson and David Hume – in the next step of his argument, in which he maintains, first, that everything in the 'natural predispositions of an organism' must have a purpose for which it is the 'most suitable and appropriate' instrument, second, that human reason is *not* as suitable an instrument for the production of happiness as mere instinct would be, so, third, the real purpose of human reason must be something other than the production of happiness altogether, namely the production of a good will. 'Since reason is not good enough to guide the will securely with respect to its objects and the satisfaction of all its needs . . . but nevertheless reason has been imparted to us as a practical faculty, i.e., as one that should have an influence on the **will**, so its true vocation must be not to serve in some other regard as a **means**, but to produce **a will that is good in itself'**

(4:396). Even if we accept Kant's claim that reason is not as good as instinct in leading to happiness, however, which might well be contested, there are still two problems with this argument. First, it is a central point of the later *Critique of the Power of Judgment* that a teleological conception of nature, that is, a conception according to which everything in nature has an end or purpose, is only a *regulative* ideal, that is, something that we can use to guide our inquiry into the mechanisms of nature, but not a *constitutive* principle, that is, a proposition that we can actually assert or use as a premise for any inference within natural science or metaphysics (see *CPJ*, especially §66, 5:376, §68, 5:381–3, and §70, 5:387–8). But then Kant should not be entitled to use the idea that everything in nature has an end for which it is best suited as the premise of a conclusive inference in moral philosophy either. At best, the thought that everything in nature has a purpose may guide us in our search for a purpose for reason other than that of leading to happiness, but it could not by itself prove that reason does have a purpose, let alone prove what that purpose is. And that brings us to the second problem with Kant's argument, namely that it relies on the unproven assumption that the production of a will that is good in itself is a genuine alternative to the production of a will that is good for something else. That is, unless it can be independently shown that the idea of a will that is good in itself apart from any end it might yield makes any sense at all, the only alternative to the idea that reason is not very good at making the will into a means for the production of happiness might be that reason is not, contrary to the teleological presupposition, good for anything at all. In other words, Kant still needs a constructive, positive argument that there can be such a thing as a will that is unconditionally good apart from any result it might produce, and that the production of such a will is the only possible goal of morality.

So let us now turn to the next stage of Kant's argument to see if it improves on what he has offered us so far.

3. ACTION FROM DUTY

Kant's next step is to claim that the common conception of the good will can be further unfolded by examining the common conception of 'duty, which contains that of a good will although under certain subjective restrictions and hindrances, which, however, far from hiding the good will and making it unrecognizable, rather accentuate it . . . and let it appear all the more brightly' (4:397). Kant's qualification that the good will appears in the form of duty because of 'certain subjective restrictions' alludes to the view, which he will emphasize later, that human beings recognize the demand of the moral law but also have inclinations that could lead them to act contrary to it, thus that we experience the demands of the moral law as a form of constraint. The assumption that we have inclinations that can conflict with the demands of morality does not play an immediate role in Kant's argument, but the difference between morally worthy action and mere action from inclination, even if that inclination is not in direct conflict with the demands of morality, certainly does. What does play a central role in Kant's argument, however, is the claim that on the common conception of duty action from inclination has no moral worth, and only action on a principle independent of all inclination does. This is what links the argument of Section I to the pre-*Groundwork* argument we considered in Chapter 2.

Kant presents his analysis of this conception of duty in a series of three propositions, although he does not formulate the first claim as explicitly as the next two, and then argues that the fundamental principle of morality, and thus the principle upon which a good will must act, follows directly from them. Kant's claim is thus that ordinary people are committed to the fundamental principle of morality as he himself understands it by their own conception of duty, even if they do not explicitly formulate this principle. Let us review the three propositions and the principle that Kant extracts from them before we consider Kant's more detailed explanation and illustration of them. The first proposition, as we glean from Kant's examples, is that an action is an expression of a good will and has moral worth only insofar as it is actually done *from duty* as its motive, not merely insofar as it is in *outward conformity* with the requirements of morality (4:398). Then, since Kant takes the motivation of acting from duty to be the alternative to acting from any ordinary desire or inclination, he also takes it that an action from duty cannot have its moral worth because it aims at any *object* of desire or inclination, but must find its moral worth in some non-object-oriented, internal principle of the will:

The second proposition is: an action from duty has its moral worth **not in the aim** that is supposed to be attained by means of it, but rather in the maxim in accordance with which it is resolved upon; thus it depends not upon the reality of the object of the action, but rather only on the **principle of the willing** in accordance with which, and without regard to all objects of the faculty of desiring, it has happened. (4:399–400)

The third proposition is then 'an inference from the previous two,' namely that '**Duty is the necessity of an action from respect for the law**' (4:400). This proposition follows from the first two because the first proposition has established that the morally worthy motivation that is an alternative to mere inclination must be a form of respect, while the second proposition has inferred that the object of a morally worthy action cannot be an object of mere inclination, and so can only be some internal law of the will; putting these two points together, the result is that the morally worthy motivation must be respect for some sort of law of volition rather than for an object of ordinary desire. As Kant puts it,

> Now since an action from duty should abstract entirely from the influence of inclination and with it from any object of the will, there remains nothing that could determine the will except objectively the **law** and subjectively **pure respect** for this practical law, hence the maxim of following this law even to the detriment of all my inclinations. (4:400–1)

But what sort of law is Kant talking about? All that we have learned so far is that mere inclination and thus desire for the object of inclination cannot be the basis for morally worthy action. Don't we need some additional information to determine what the moral law can be? Kant recognizes that this is the natural question to ask, but claims that we do not need anything more to figure out what the moral law actually is:

> But what sort of law can that be, the representation of which, even without regard to the effect expected from it, must determine the will, so that this can be called good absolutely and without restriction? Since I have robbed the will of every impulse that could arise for it from following any law, nothing remains but the universal lawfulness of actions in general, which alone can serve the will as a principle, i.e., I should never conduct myself except

in such a way **that I could also will that my maxim should become a universal law**. Here mere lawfulness in general (not grounded on a law determined by certain actions) now serves the will as a principle and must so serve it if duty is not to be an empty delusion and chimerical concept; and common human understanding is in complete agreement with this in its practical judging, and always has this principle before its eyes. (4:402)

Kant's claim is that the only alternative to adopting as one's principle of action (we will discuss his technical concept of 'maxims' later) a law always to seek some particular object of inclination is simply to make it one's general principle to act in accordance with the idea of law or lawfulness in general; and since this idea is nothing but the idea of universal validity, this requirement is to act only on particular principles that could also be universal laws, that is, to act only on principles that everyone else could also accept and act upon. That is in fact the test that he claims everyone faced with a moral issue or dilemma actually applies to their proposed course of action. To have a good will is thus simply to be committed to acting only upon principles that could also be universal laws, to act in accordance with duty is to act only upon such laws even in the face of our normal human temptations to do otherwise, and to act from duty is to be motivated and remain committed always to act in accordance with duty from nothing but respect for this requirement.

Obviously we will have to consider carefully Kant's claim that the requirement that we act only upon principles that could also be universal laws is identical with the fundamental principle of morality; but since Kant refines and expands upon this formulation in Section II of the *Groundwork*, we can defer our scrutiny of it until the next chapter. For now, let us see how Kant supports the three propositions about duty that he has claimed lead to the moral law. Kant devotes the bulk of his argument to support for the first proposition that only action from duty, not even action in accord with duty, is morally worthy and evidence of a good will. He argues this claim by considering one class of actions, namely actions that could be motivated either by the thought of duty or by some immediate inclination. There are two other classes of action that might be considered, namely those that are actually contrary to duty and those that might be consistent with duty but toward which we have no immediate inclination at all, but do only because they are means to some other end for which we do have an immediate inclination (4:397). Kant does not consider these kinds of actions because nobody could think that they have any moral worth. He does not mention the case of actions that are actually in conflict with the demands of morality but are performed because their agents sincerely but mistakenly *think* that they are required by morality; some might think that actions of this kind have moral worth, or at least show that the characters of their agents have moral worth even if their particular actions do not. Rather, what Kant considers is the case of actions that are in outward compliance with the demands of morality but could be performed either from an immediate inclination to do so *or* because their agents recognize that these actions are what morality requires and are motivated to perform them by that thought alone. What Kant claims is that while actions that are in outward compliance with the demands of morality should always be encouraged, it is only those actions that are motivated by the thought that they are what morality demands that are morally worthy and evidence of a will that is unconditionally good, that is, good in all circumstances. He argues this by means of a thought-experiment: imagine people who are naturally inclined to perform types of action that are required by duty, then imagine that for some reason they lose that inclination but perform the actions anyway solely because they recognize that to do so is their duty; then you will realize that only in the latter case have they demonstrated possession of an unconditionally good will, a will that is good regardless of circumstances including their own inclinations, and thus that their actions and characters are morally worthy. From this it will also follow that the principle on which a morally good will acts must not depend upon the presence of any inclination, which is the conclusion Kant is really driving at. (It is important to see that Kant's examples are thought-experiments because in Section II of the *Groundwork* he will insist that it is not safe to found moral theories on *actual examples* of human behavior, because in real life there may always be hidden motives of self-interest; but in thought-experiments the agents have no motives except the ones we assign them, so this problem does not arise. Nor can our responses to thought-experiments be distorted by *our own* hidden motives of self-interest, because since the agents are not real we do not stand in any actual relations to them and do not stand to benefit from their imaginary actions in any way.)

Kant offers four examples to make his point, one of which is a case in which the agent has an ulterior motive but not an immediate inclination to perform a dutiful action, which nobody would confuse with morally worthy action, while the other three are examples of actions that could be done either from immediate inclination or from duty, but have moral worth only in the latter case. (These examples anticipate the four classes of duties that Kant will use to confirm his formulations of the categorical imperative in Section II of the *Groundwork*, although he does not mention that point.) The first example Kant considers is that of the 'prudent merchant' who never overcharges even his most inexperienced customers, not because he is moved either by the thought of his duty or by any immediate inclination of love for his customers, but because he believes that honesty is literally the best policy, that is, that he will get more customers and thus become richer if he is widely known not to overcharge. This is a matter of sheer self-interest, and while nobody would think there is anything wrong with such a merchant's policy – after all, no one is being harmed by it – neither would anyone think that there is anything morally meritorious about it, or that it is evidence of any good will on the part of the merchant.

The second example that Kant considers is the duty 'to preserve one's life' or not to commit suicide. The morality of suicide was a lively theme in eighteenth-century thought, popularized first by Joseph Addison's tragedy *Cato* (1713), about the Roman patrician and general who committed suicide rather than accept the dictatorship of Julius Caesar, and then by Johann Wolfgang von Goethe's immensely popular novella *The Sorrows of Young Werther* (1774), about a passionate young man who commits suicide rather than accepting the unavailability of his beloved.[1] Kant will argue in Section II that suicide, or at least suicide from the motive of self-love (the desire to avoid one's own suffering), is always immoral. Here, however, his point is that people ordinarily have a powerful immediate inclination in favor of the preservation of their own life, so that when they refrain from suicide, as they almost always do, they are doing the right thing but are demonstrating no special moral motivation. However, if we imagine someone whose 'taste for life has been entirely removed by adversities and hopeless grief' yet who nevertheless refrains from suicide, then we must conclude that such a person is motivated 'neither by inclination nor by fear, but solely from duty,' and in that case we would 'assign his maxim a moral content'

(4:398). Kant's implication is that our common response to this example shows that we regard motivation from duty rather than by inclination as morally worthy evidence of a good will: our commitment to preserve our own life is not contingent upon things going well and thus upon an inclination to keep enjoying a good life, but is unconditional.

Kant's next example concerns our duty of beneficence toward others, that is, the duty not merely not to injure them but actually to assist them in realizing their own goals. Here Kant claims that while it is certainly in conformity with duty and 'lovable' for someone to be beneficent to others because he has a 'sympathetic' soul and enjoys an 'inner gratification' in helping others, that is, has an immediate inclination to help others which he gratifies by actually helping them, and such a person should hardly be discouraged but rather deserves 'praise and encouragement,' there is actually nothing morally meritorious in such a person, because he is really acting only for his own gratification. But now imagine that such a person's sympathetic inclinations are wiped out by his own troubles, but that he nevertheless continues to assist others to the full extent of his capacities: then it would be clear that his good will is not dependent upon his own circumstances, but is unconditional, thus that he performs the beneficent action 'without any inclination, solely from duty,' and then it would 'first have its genuine moral worth' (4:398). Again, this is supposed to be our common response to imagining such a case: we are all supposed to value action from duty in a way that we do not value action from inclination.

Kant's final case concerns the duty 'to secure one's own happiness' (4:399). The moral significance of one's own happiness is a difficult issue for Kant, and his discussion here is particularly involuted. His initial suggestion that the duty to secure one's own happiness is 'indirect' is explained by the fact that 'lack of contentment with one's own condition,' or unhappiness, 'could readily become a great **temptation to the transgression of duties**'; that is, dissatisfaction with one's lot could easily tempt one to attempt to improve it by impermissible means, such as theft rather than honest toil. But Kant does not develop that thought here.[2] Rather, he makes the following argument. First, he supposes that 'all human beings already have of themselves the most powerful and inmost inclination to happiness, precisely because in this idea all inclinations are united into a sum,' that is, because the idea of one's own happiness is in fact nothing

45

other than the idea of the maximum possible gratification of the sum of one's inclinations. It is in fact because we must, by this definition, have an inclination toward our own happiness that Kant supposes the promotion of our own happiness could not be a duty, because a duty is something morally requisite that we may have to be constrained to pursue against our inclination.[3] But, Kant next argues, it is never possible to satisfy *all* of our inclinations – for example, a sufferer from gout cannot satisfy both his inclination to have some more port tonight and to be free of pain tomorrow – and the indeterminate idea of happiness as the satisfaction of some maximum number of our inclinations cannot by itself tell us which of our incompatible inclinations we can gratify and which we must suppress. Then Kant concludes that 'if the general inclination toward happiness does not determine' one's will in favor of one inclination rather than another, 'there still remains here, as in all other cases, a law, namely to promote [one's] happiness not out of inclination, but out of duty, and then [one's] conduct first has its genuine moral worth' (4:399). Kant's conclusion is out of kilter: even if one can see that promoting one's own happiness is a duty after all, which Kant has not here explained, knowing that one's own happiness is a duty and being moved by that fact to promote it is not going to help one when one is torn between two incompatible inclinations the gratification of each of which seems necessary to one's happiness, like the gouty man's desire for another drink tonight yet for good health in the morning. One still needs some way to make the conception of happiness determinate enough to resolve such a conflict, which the mere idea that even one's own happiness can be a duty does not provide. The case Kant should have considered here is rather what ancients called *akrasia* or weakness of the will, that is, the case in which one knows perfectly well what would make one happy all things considered but still is not inclined to do it; that's the case in which the thought that one has a duty toward one's own happiness could provide the motivation that mere inclination cannot. However, if we overlook this difficulty in Kant's argument, we can still accept his general point in all these examples, namely that there is no unconditional moral value in pursuing a morally permissible or even a morally mandatory objective out of mere inclination. Such value lies only in pursuing it from the motive of duty itself, which is not dependent upon the contingent state of one's current inclinations and is in that way unconditional.

Kant's claim that inclination is not a morally worthy motivation has led to a long history of controversy. We will discuss that shortly, but let us first examine the remaining steps of Kant's argument. These depend upon the conclusion to which these examples are supposed to have led us, namely that there is no moral value in acting upon inclination, but only in acting from duty. The basis for Kant's second proposition, as we saw, is that since there is no moral value in acting from inclination, the desirability of any particular *objects* of inclination cannot be the basis of the fundamental moral principle. His brief discussion of this proposition prepares the way for the conclusion of the whole argument of Section I by setting up the alternatives that are supposedly available for the determination of the will. Either the will is determined by some inclination to pursue some particular object of desire, or it must adopt a principle that is entirely 'without regard to any ends that could be effected through [our] action'; the will is always at a crossroads where it must choose between 'its *a priori* principle, which is formal,' and 'its *a posteriori* incentives, which are material.' But since the moral will does not act out of inclination, as has been seen in the discussion of the first proposition, it then has no choice but to act in accordance with 'the formal principle of willing in general . . . because it has been deprived of any material principle' (4:400). The key assumption that Kant is making here is that the only possible ends of action are those that are suggested by inclination, so that the only alternative to acting from inclination is to act on a formal principle that makes no reference to ends at all. This is the premise that allows Kant to conclude from the whole argument that the only possible law for the morally worthy and unconditionally good will is the formal law that one should act only on maxims that could also be universal laws (4:402).

But if Kant's argument rests on the assumption that the only two alternatives for the determination of the will are either mere conditionally valuable ends suggested by mere inclinations or the purely formal law to act only on generalizable principles, then his argument is formally unsound, for it has left out one possibility, namely that there might be a *necessary* end of some kind, that is, an end the pursuit of which is commanded by something other than merely contingent inclination, and thus that the will has the choice between pursuing merely conditionally valuable ends or pursuing this unconditionally valuable end rather than the choice between pursuing contingent ends and conforming to a principle that has nothing to do with ends at all. Does this apparent omission in Kant's argument doom his entire moral theory to failure even before it has left the starting-blocks? We will see in the next chapter that it does not, because Kant's argument in Section II of the *Groundwork* does nothing less than ground the obligatory force of the law that we should act only on universalizable principles in the unconditional value of an end in itself. In other words, he will ground his entire argument on the supposition that there is a necessary end after all, and that the choice that the will faces in any situation calling for a moral choice is precisely the choice between pursuing some merely contingent and conditionally valuable end or acting in behalf of an end that is necessary and unconditionally valuable. His argument in Section II will be that we can pursue that necessary end only *through* the adoption of the formal law to act only on universalizable principles.

We will have to consider the details of that argument later. For now we might only ask why Kant sets up his argument in Section I in a way that is formally unsound and does not do justice to the more powerful argument that he will develop in Section II. The answer to this question may simply be that Section I is supposed to remain at the level of common conceptions of morality, and that Kant thinks that the idea of the merely conditional value of ends suggested by inclination is obvious to common sense but that the idea of a necessary end is not, so that the introduction of the latter idea will have to wait until the exposition shifts to a more philosophical plane. At the same time, as we shall shortly see, Kant holds that common sense does in fact always use the test of the universalizability of its principles when faced with a moral dilemma, so he may have assumed that common sense would acknowledge not only the starting point of his argument, that is, the merely conditional value of ends suggested by inclination, but also its end-point, namely, the requirement of universalizibility, without worrying about how to get from one to the other.

Before we turn to Kant's claim that common-sense morality does employ the principle to which his argument is supposed to lead and to the debate about Kant's underlying premise that there is no moral worth in being motivated by contingent inclination, let us look at his third proposition in a little more detail. Remember that this proposition, that the subjective state of respect for the objectively valid formal law of the will is the only morally worthy motivation, is supposed to follow simply from the combination of the first two propositions. This means that it too should depend upon the premise that there is no moral worth in being motivated by mere inclination. And that it does quickly becomes evident, for what Kant says in support of this proposition is this:

> For the object as the effect of my proposed action I can certainly have **inclination**, but never **respect**, just because it is an effect and not the activity of a will. Likewise I cannot have respect for inclination in general, whether it be my own or that of someone else, I can at most approve of it in the first case, in the second case sometimes even love it, i.e., regard it as favorable to my own advantage. Only that which is connected with my will merely as ground, but never as effect, what does not serve my inclination but outweighs it, or at least entirely excludes it from being calculated into my choice, hence only the mere law for itself can be an object of respect and hereby a command. (4:400)

What this passage suggests is that common moral sense will recognize that only a genuine action of the will, not something that merely happens *to* the will, is a proper object of moral evaluation at all, whether positive or negative, and thus that inclination, precisely because it is just a natural occurrence that merely happens in the human being, cannot be the proper basis for moral evaluation. That is why no inclination, no matter how sympathetic or amiable, can be the basis for the moral worth of the good will: it is not a product of the will at all. Instead, Kant supposes, continuing to use the contrast upon which he has relied in his argument for the second proposition, the only alternative to pursuing an object of inclination is for the will to take the action of choosing to follow 'mere law for itself,' that is, to act only on universalizable principles. That decision to respect the moral law is itself the only thing that is truly worthy of respect because it is the only way in which the will can truly be active rather than passive.

Several comments are called for here. First, if the present analysis of Kant's argument is correct, then it rests on a fundamental and undemonstrated, perhaps indemonstrable, *normative* premise, namely that only a genuine action of the will is worthy of moral respect. Kant's argument works by combining this normative premise with the further claims that being moved by inclination is not a genuine action of the will at all and that choosing to act on a purely formal law is the only alternative to being passively moved by inclination. The claim that being moved by inclination is not a genuine action of the will might be regarded as a normatively neutral, purely metaphysical claim; but Kant's present argument does not depend only upon that claim, but also upon the normative premise that only a genuine action of the will is worthy of moral respect. This premise may be regarded as the positive form of Kant's earlier thesis that there is nothing more irksome than being pushed around by inclinations, although it is now offered as a normative rather than psychological claim. Thus the present argument cannot be considered as an argument that derives a normative conclusion – the fundamental principle of morality – from purely metaphysical premises. It can only get off the ground by making at least one normative assumption, which is supposed to be a common-sensical one about moral evaluation. We will have to see whether this conclusion also applies to Kant's more philosophical derivation of the categorical imperative later in the *Groundwork*.

The second point we should note here is that Kant's premise that inclination is not a proper object of moral evaluation because it is not an action of the will at all implies that the mere occurrence of inclination is not a ground for either negative or positive moral evaluation, and that negative as well as positive moral evaluation must always be addressed to a genuine action of the will – to the character of an agent's choice, not to the character of his or her inclinations *per se*. Kant does not bring this point out in the *Groundwork*, but it is central to his argument in the First Book of *Religion within the Boundaries of Mere Reason*. Here Kant explicitly says that since the 'subjective ground' of either goodness or evil must 'itself always be a deed of freedom,' 'the ground of evil' as well as of good 'cannot lie in any object *determining* the power of choice through inclination, nor in any natural impulses, but only in a rule that the power of choice itself produces for the exercise of its freedom.'[4] Indeed, appealing once again to his teleological assumption that we should always assume, at least until proven otherwise, that everything in nature has its good and proper use, Kant actually argues, against puritans and ascetics of all kind, that we should assume that natural impulses or inclinations are a force for the good, unless they are misused.[5] Instead, Kant argues in the *Religion*, whether people are good or evil always depends upon what choices they make, thus upon their free decisions whether and when to act upon particular inclinations: 'The human being must make or have made **himself** into whatever he is or should become in a moral sense, good or evil. These two must be an effect of his free power of choice, for otherwise they could not be imputed to him and . . . he could be neither **morally** good nor evil.'[6] Specifically, Kant argues, the will has the choice between two principles or fundamental maxims: it can choose to make the moral law 'the **supreme condition**' of the satisfaction of any particular inclinations it may happen to have, or it may choose conversely to subordinate the moral law to the principle of self-love, that is, the maxim always to gratify one's own inclinations whether doing so is consistent with fulfilling the demands of morality or not.[7]

This means that choosing to act on the moral law is not exactly the alternative to being determined by inclination; it is more precisely the alternative to *choosing* to be guided by inclination. If we accept Kant's premises that having inclinations is not by itself a proper subject for moral evaluation at all, but that moral evaluation must always be of an act of the will, and that there are two moral evaluations of action that are always possible, namely that it is either good or evil, this is a natural way for him to model human action, although it will cause a problem for Kant's key argument in Section III of the *Groundwork*. We do not have to worry about that yet, however. For the moment we can just accept the positive side of Kant's argument in Section I, namely that since inclinations are not acts of the will at all, the proper basis for a positive moral evaluation of an action or an agent cannot be the presence of any inclination, but rather a commitment of the will to act in accordance with the moral law. It is in this sense that respect for the moral law is the only possible expression of the good will, and, when that respect occurs in the face of some opposing inclination, the only possible expression of duty.

The final stage of Kant's argument in Section I is his defense of the claim that 'common human reason' in fact always uses the principle that one should act only on principles that one could also will to be universal law in its 'practical judging' (4:402). Kant says that any normal person, considering for example whether it might be permissible to get out of a jam by 'making a promise with the intention of not keeping it,' distinguishes between the question of whether it would be *prudent* to do so, that is, whether he could successfully get away with it, and the question of whether it would be *in conformity with duty* to do so. Prudence, everyone will recognize, usually argues against making the false promise, because usually one cannot be sure that one will get away with it; but sometimes one could be sure of that, and then prudence has nothing to say against making such a promise. But the answer to the question of duty, everyone will also recognize, is not contingent upon circumstances like that. Rather,

> In order to instruct myself . . . with regard to the solution to the problem of whether a lying promise is in conformity with duty, I ask myself: whether I would be satisfied if my maxim (of getting myself out of embarrassment by a dishonest promise) should hold as a universal law (for myself as well as for others), and whether I could say to myself that anyone may make a dishonest promise if he finds himself in an embarrassment from which he cannot extract himself in any other way? Then I quickly realize that I can, to be sure, will the lie, but not a universal law to lie; for in accordance with the latter there really would be no promises at all, because it would be in vain to pledge my will with regard to my future actions to others who would not believe this pledge, or, if they rashly did so, would pay me back in the same coin, and hence my maxim, as soon as it were made into a universal law, must destroy itself. (4:403)

Kant's claim is that anyone considering the dutifulness of a course of action would ask whether he could successfully act that way if everyone else did as well, and that everyone raises this question not because they have explicitly formulated the moral law as Kant has but because they nevertheless tacitly recognize that law. If a person then realizes that she could not successfully act in a certain way if everyone else did too, but could only act upon that way if others did not, then she will recognize that her action is morally corrupt: it could work only if she were to be an exception from general law. In this case, the person's plan of getting out of trouble by making a false promise would not work if everyone made false promises, because if that were known to be the case then no one in her right mind would accept anyone's promise to begin with – the words 'I promise to . . .' would just be hot air. Kant's claim is that this is the common pattern of moral reasoning that confirms his analysis of duty.

Kant is not assuming as a matter of empirical fact that one person's making a false promise would in fact lead everybody else to start making false promises and thereby undermine the practice of promising. Whether that would actually happen would depend upon whether one's own intentions actually became known to everyone else, whether others thought that one's own behavior actually gave them good reason to pay the first liar back in his own coin, and so on. Those are all contingent matters. Rather, Kant says we just ask whether we *could* successfully act in a certain way *if* everyone else also acted that way; *whether* our acting this way would actually lead others to do the same is irrelevant to this question. Kant's assumption is that the moral agent wills to act only upon principles that *could* also be universal laws, and that if she realizes that her proposed principle could not also be a universal law, that is, that she could not act upon it if everyone else also chose to do so – whether or not her choice has anything to do with their choosing to do so – then she would not will to act upon it.

Kant will provide further illustrations of how the principle of acting only upon principles that could also be universal laws is supposed to work in Section II of the *Groundwork*, and we can leave critical scrutiny of whether this principle really works in all and only the cases in which it should until the next chapter. For now, the question to be asked is only whether the pattern of moral reasoning that Kant has described seems to be one that ordinary people actually use, even if they have never read the *Groundwork* or explicitly formulated the principle as Kant has. If that seems plausible, then Kant has all he needs for the moment.

4. CRITICAL ISSUES IN *GROUNDWORK* I

Let us now consider some critical issues about Kant's argument in Section I. Kant's insistence that true good will and moral worth are demonstrated only in action from the motivation of respect for duty, not action from inclination has often been met with abhorrence, for two different reasons. On the one hand, the idea that we should find greater moral value in an agent who acts from a sense of duty than in one who acts from sympathetic feelings has seemed to many a cold and heartless picture of human virtue. Friedrich Schiller gave inimitable voice to this criticism early on, although in fact his intention was to lampoon the clumsy interpretation of Kant by his critics rather than Kant himself:

Gladly I serve my friends, but alas I do it with pleasure.
Hence I am plagued with doubt that I am not a virtuous person.
Surely your only resource is to try to despise them entirely,
And then with aversion to do what your duty enjoins you.[8]

But the same objection has been at the root of many modern criticisms of Kant, such as Michael Stocker's claim that someone who goes to visit a sick friend out of a sense of duty rather than directly from feelings of friendship undermines the point of her visit, and Bernard Williams's claim that a man who saves his drowning wife rather than an unfortunate stranger in the same danger out of a sense of duty rather than immediately from his conjugal love has 'one thought too many.'[9] The other reason, expressed not so much in serious commentary on Kant but in general criticism of German philosophy during the World Wars of the twentieth century, is the idea that Kant's position justifies *any* action as long as it is done out of a sense of duty: thus, the soldier or party member who commits the most heinous crimes because he believes it is his duty to follow any orders given by his superiors is supposed to be a genuine example of Kant's conception of an agent acting from respect for duty.

Both of these objections fail, and for the same reason: they fail to recognize that Kant's examples of agents who act out of respect for duty without any sympathetic inclinations at all are thought-experiments designed to help us correctly identify the fundamental principle of morality, and are not intended to offer a complete picture of human virtue. Kant's point is that since a person undeniably demonstrates good will and moral worth in the case in which he or she acts morally even in the absence of all inclination to do so, thus by elimination from no other motive than respect for duty alone, the fundamental principle of morality must be one that makes no reference to inclination and does not depend upon the presence of inclination for its efficacy. But this does not mean that any action from a sense of duty no matter how misguided is morally worthy, nor that the only morally worthy action is that which is actually performed from respect for duty in the absence of all other inclinations.

The first point is easy to see: the soldier or party hack who thinks it is his duty simply to do whatever his superior commands has obviously not thought about the concept of duty at all, for if he had he would have realized that it cannot be his duty to act on a mere impulse of his superior (or of his superior's superior on up the line to the Führer or Great Leader) any more than it could be his duty to act merely on his own impulses; he has not recognized that action on duty is not identical with action on anyone's mere impulse, but can only be to act on a principle that all could accept regardless of their impulses, a condition that will surely not be satisfied by the orders he is following. The second point, that Kant is not actually praising or recommending action done from respect for the genuine principle of duty but in the absence of all feeling, is perhaps harder to see. But a careful study of Kant's various remarks about the relation between feeling and duty will show that while in *Groundwork* I Kant uses the thought-experiment of agents who were first motivated *only* by sympathetic inclination but then lost that inclination entirely and so could be motivated only by respect for the moral law in order to show that the moral law itself is independent from inclination, when he discusses the actual nature of human virtue he assumes both that respect for duty is typically *accompanied* with a general moral feeling, what we might think of as a feeling of warmth in the cause of virtue, and that in real life one's general commitment to duty, which is accompanied with this general moral feeling, works precisely by allowing one to act on particular sympathetic inclinations in appropriate circumstances, and even by leading one to cultivate such feelings, while requiring one not to act on certain other feelings or even not to act on ordinarily beneficial feelings in particular circumstances in which that would be morally inappropriate. In other words, Kant's actual model of virtuous human behavior is far more complex than his examples in *Groundwork* I, which are designed only to elucidate the general principle of morality, might be taken to suggest if their role is misunderstood and inflated: Kant's real picture is that one's commitment to the moral law at the deepest level of one's will is reflected in a general feeling of warmth in the cause of virtue and displays its efficacy by causing one to cultivate and act upon certain particular inclinations in certain circumstances and to suppress or not act upon those or other inclinations in other circumstances.

We will have to go beyond *Groundwork* I in order to appreciate this point. But in order to clarify what is at stake here, let us first consider some recent discussion of this issue. Barbara Herman points in the right direction in 'On the Value of Acting from the Motive of Duty.'[10] She criticizes the proposal of another commentator, Richard Henson, who had suggested that we could understand Kant's examples in *Groundwork* I as offering a 'battle-citation' model of judgments of moral worth, according to which virtuous agents deserve commendation because they have had to overcome either a sheer lack of all inclination or inclinations contrary to duty in order to do what they know is their duty, but that later Kant had suggested a 'fitness-report' model of moral evaluation, according to which agents are judged to be virtuous as long as we think that they have a commitment to do their duty that *would* have caused them to perform their duty *if* an inclination to do so had been lacking, but which does not need to have actually been efficacious if inclinations to do what is the right thing had actually been present.[11] Herman's objection to Henson is that neither his interpretation of Kant's *Groundwork* examples nor of his later examples is correct, because in both cases what Kant requires is and is only that an agent's fundamental *principle* not be simply to act on his inclinations, however morally beneficial or not they may be and however strong or weak they be, but to act as duty requires. Herman maintains that 'What the motive of duty provides is a commitment to do what you want only if the maxim of your action is judged morally satisfactory,'[12] or a 'limiting condition'[13] on your other motives, a general principle that gives permission to act upon inclinations that are consistent with or conducive to doing what duty requires but prohibits you from acting on inclinations that would lead to actions inconsistent with duty. This idea of the moral principle as a 'limiting condition' then offers a way to answer such objections as those of Michael Stocker or Bernard Williams: the friend who is simply inclined toward visiting her friend in the hospital does not have to consciously think that to do so is her duty, let alone let her friend know that she thinks this, which is what would be so disturbing to the friend if he thought that were her only motive for visiting him; she simply has to have a general commitment to doing things to which she is inclined, like visiting her sick friend, only as long as doing so is consistent with duty, for example as long as she does not have some other commitment that is morally more urgent. Likewise, the husband in Bernard Williams's case does not have to consciously think that to save his wife is his moral duty before trying to save her, which would be the disturbing 'one thought too many'; he only needs to have a general commitment to doing his duty such that he would not save his wife if he had some even more pressing duty to fulfill, say saving a drowning doctor who is the only one with the vaccine to save millions of people.

Herman's idea of the principle always to do your duty as a general, or we might say 'second-order', principle which governs your action on particular inclinations, points in the right direction, but does not capture all of Kant's thought about the relation between duty and feeling. She does not emphasize that in Kant's view a person's commitment to this general principle is itself expressed by the presence of a distinctive moral feeling, nor that it does not merely *license* acting upon some inclinations in some circumstances while rejecting others, but typically *works through* certain inclinations and indeed actually requires us to *cultivate* certain kinds of feelings that will be efficacious in leading us to do what morality requires in the actual conditions of human life. Let us now turn briefly to some of Kant's later comments about duty and feeling in order to illustrate these two points. The first point is that Kant does not treat our general commitment to do what duty requires purely as an abstract, second-order commitment, but also insists that it is accompanied by a special moral feeling. His commitment to this view appears in several forms over the course of his writings in moral philosophy. In the *Groundwork*, Kant typically uses the word 'respect' (*Achtung*) to mean simply the choice to make the moral law one's own fundamental maxim: for example, in the statement of the third proposition in the analysis of the common concept of duty in Section I, Kant uses the word in such phrases as 'respect for duty' or '**pure respect** for the moral law' (4:400) to characterize an agent's choice and commitment to act as the moral law requires without any connotation of a specific affective or emotional aspect to that choice and commitment. However, he says in Section II that

> the pure representation of duty and in general of the moral law, mixed with no alien additive from empirical stimuli, has through reason alone (which hereby first becomes aware that it can also be practical of itself) an influence on the human heart that is so much more powerful than all other incentives that one might offer from the empirical realm that in the consciousness of its dignity it despises the latter and becomes their master. (4:410–11).

Here Kant describes a conscious effect 'on the human heart' of the representation of duty through which we become aware of the power of pure practical reason and which expresses our contempt of empirical incentives as moral motives and is part of our mastery over such incentives. By saying that pure reason produces this effect 'on the human heart,' Kant is implying that what he previously called 'pure respect' for the moral law has an emotional dimension, and that this emotional dimension is part of the mechanism by means of which non-moral incentives are mastered. Kant does not call this emotional dimension itself a feeling of respect in the *Groundwork*, but that is precisely what he does in the *Critique of Practical Reason* when he writes this:

> The moral law strikes down self-conceit. But since this law is still something positive in itself, namely the form of an intellectual causality, i.e., of freedom, while in opposition to the subjective antagonist, namely the inclinations in us, it **weakens** self-conceit, it is at the same time an object of **respect**, and when it **tramples**, i.e., humiliates self-conceit, an object of the greatest **respect**, hence also the ground of a positive feeling, which is not of empirical origin and is known *a priori*. (*PracR*, 5:73)

Here Kant says that pure respect for the law produces a complex effect on our emotions, a painful one insofar as it (at least sometimes) requires us to strike down self-conceit, that is, our disposition to act on our own inclinations as if gratifying them were the most important thing we could do, but also a positive one insofar as we have a feeling of the power of our reason to do this and the rightness of so doing. Kant also calls this mixed but in the end positive state of our emotions or feelings itself 'respect' when he continues that 'respect for the moral law is a feeling, which is effected by an intellectual ground, and this feeling is the only one that we cognize entirely *a priori* and into the necessity of which we have insight' (*loc. cit.*). In other words, respect for the moral law in the intellectual or abstract sense produces a feeling of respect, an emotional state of which we are aware, which is its usual concomitant and part of the mechanism through which it acts upon our other incentives. Thus Kant's model of the virtuous person is hardly exhausted by the image of the formerly sympathetic philanthropist who now feels nothing at all but nevertheless somehow forces himself to continue to fulfill his philanthropic duty through some sheer act of will; in real life, Kant supposes, the act of will to perform one's duty will be accompanied with a subjective feeling, and it may be through that feeling that the will overpowers any refractory inclinations that an agent may have. This may not fit the ideal of a friend or lover who acts on sheer feeling without any thought of duty at all, but neither is it an image of a person who cold-heartedly does what duty requires moved solely by the abstract thought that he is doing his duty.

But this is still only part of Kant's analysis of the affective or emotional aspects of moral motivation. The second part of his account is that we are disposed to particular feelings, for example feelings of sympathy toward other human beings in a state of suffering and need, and that what our general commitment to morality requires is precisely that we act upon these feelings in appropriate circumstances and even cultivate them so that they will be available to us to act upon in such circumstances. In his eagerness to argue that the fundamental principle of morality itself cannot be derived from or grounded upon inclinations, Kant sometimes obscures this point. But his considered position is rather what he says in his discussion of 'duties of love' such as beneficence, gratitude, and sympathy in the 'Doctrine of Virtue' of the *Metaphysics of Morals*:

> **Sympathetic joy** and **compassion** [*Mitfreude* and *Mitleid*, literally 'joy with' and 'suffering with' others] (*sympathia moralis*) are to be sure sensory feelings (therefore called aesthetic) of pleasure or displeasure at the condition of gratification or suffering of others (shared feeling, sympathetic sentiment), the susceptibility to which has been implanted in human beings by nature. But to use these as the means for the promotion of an active and rational benevolence is still a particular although only conditional duty under the name of **humanity** (*humanitas*): for here the human being is considered not merely as a rational being, but as an animal endowed with reason. (*MM*, 'Doctrine of Virtue,' §34, 6:456)

Kant's contrast here between a merely 'rational being' and an 'animal endowed with reason' is telling: perhaps if we were purely rational beings without emotions at all, we would be moved to action by some sort of purely intellectual apprehension of the moral law; but we are not such beings, we are animals with an emotional life, and in us the general commitment to the moral works by using particular feelings that we have as springs or triggers to particular actions. That is, our general commitment to the moral law, itself manifested to us through the general moral feeling or feeling of respect, often works *through* particular feelings such as feelings of compassion as well. Moreover, Kant adds, even though nature has implanted in us a disposition or susceptibility to have such feelings, we must actively preserve and cultivate them out of or as part of our general commitment to do our duty; that is, it is part of our duty to take steps to ensure that we will have the particular feelings that will enable us to do our duty on particular occasions. Thus Kant writes that it is an 'indirect duty to cultivate the compassionate natural (aesthetic) feelings in us and to utilize them as so many means to sympathy from moral principles' and the feeling appropriate to them. For example,

> It is duty not to avoid the places where the poor who lack the most necessary things are to be found, but to seek them out, and not to flee sickrooms or debtors' prisons in order to eradicate the painful sympathetic feeling that one might not be able to avoid: for this is a stimulus that has been implanted in us by nature in order to do that which the representation of duty might not be able to arrange by itself alone. (*MM*, 'Doctrine of Virtue,' §35, 6:457)

The very last clause of this quotation might make it sound as if we need sympathetic feelings as a fall-back in case our motivation to do our duty for its own sake is not strong enough, and that it is for this reason that we must avoid suppressing these feelings (by fleeing sickrooms) and take active steps to cultivate them (by seeking out those who need our help). But it is more consistent with Kant's previous statements that these sorts of feelings are the means that nature has implanted in us to do our duty to suppose that we typically perform our duties by acting upon feelings which have themselves been preserved and cultivated on the basis of our general commitment to morality. In other words, the general commitment to duty, which is itself accompanied and made efficacious by the feeling of respect, causes us to cultivate particular feelings which then prompt us to act as duty requires in particular circumstances.

This may seem like a complicated picture of moral motivation, but one thing that is important about it is that it does not leave the presence and efficacy of feelings such as sympathy, love, or friendship up to chance, but rather emphasizes that the virtuous person actually cultivates such feelings. In fact, such cultivation may take two forms: Kant's example of visiting the poor and sick suggests that we must work to cultivate general feelings of sympathy, but we may also have to cultivate feelings that will lead us to fulfill our duties toward particular persons, or in contemporary parlance 'work on our relationships.' Kant does not emphasize the latter point in the 'Doctrine of Virtue,' but in his discussion of marriage in some of his lectures, Kant emphasizes that in a marriage there is a moral duty of spouses to cultivate respect toward one another precisely so that they will still treat each other well even when 'love from inclination' based merely on 'instinctual attractions, such as beauty or talent,' fades away or even disappears.[14] An ethics of mere inclination would in fact be very unreliable: it is easy enough to imagine that in the throes of first love, a young husband might be and be expected to be moved to save his wife from sheer passion, but over a long relationship there might well be times when he had better be moved by the thought that he has a duty toward his wife, because the kind of passion people might have when they first know each other cannot always be counted upon. Over the long term, successful relationships, no matter how passionate they may be at moments, must be grounded in a firm sense of duty.

Before we leave the topic of duty and feeling, there is one final point to consider. Note that in the passage from his discussion of the duty to use sympathetic feelings as means to moral ends, Kant says that the duty to use such feelings is not only 'particular' but also 'conditional.' What does he mean by the latter term? He could mean that it is a duty to act upon sympathetic feelings only insofar as a matter of empirical fact they are the means that nature has given us to make it possible for us to do our duty – nature might have constituted our psychology quite otherwise, in which case we would not have this indirect duty. But he must also mean that we should act on these feelings only subject to the condition that the actions they would lead us to perform in particular circumstances are in fact the actions that duty permits or requires in those circumstances; in other words, we do have to use the general principle of morality as a limiting condition on our disposition to act upon particular feelings, no matter how generally consistent with morality they are, even though the role of limiting condition is not, as we have seen, the only role that commitment to the general principle of morality plays. For example, your general disposition to help people struggling with heavy burdens should not lead you to lend a hand to someone struggling to load a large package into a van outside of your favorite art museum in the middle of the night, because that person might be in the middle of stealing a valuable work of art, in which case your duty is not to help him but to call the police.[15] It is easy to imagine circumstances in which even what are ordinarily the most valuable feelings for the fulfillment of our duties could lead to actions contrary to duty. So it is our duty not only to cultivate such feelings as means to the performance of our duty, but also to make sure that we act upon them only when that is consistent with duty. Knowing that will not always require conscious reflection, but sometimes it may, and in such cases our duty will include the duty to reflect on our circumstances and the permissibility of acting upon our feelings. This is another important point that an ethics of pure inclination seems to leave out.

Let us conclude this chapter by returning to Kant's original idea of the unconditional value of freedom. As I have suggested, the assumption of the fundamental value of freedom is at work in Section I in the form of Kant's claim that action out of mere inclination has no genuine moral worth because it is something that merely happens to a person, not a genuinely willed action of the person, or, in other words, a genuinely free action. Kant's supposition, in other words, is that only a genuinely free action has moral value.

To be sure, this proposition is not identical to the proposition that the freedom of an action is itself the fundamental *source* of its moral worthiness; it might be merely a *necessary condition* for ascribing worthiness to an action or an agent. That is, it might be possible to suppose that an action derives its value from the end it is intended and designed to realize, but that a person deserves no moral praise or credit for performing such an action unless he has performed it freely or voluntarily rather than being compelled or tricked, whether by natural forces or other people, into performing it. Does Kant have an argument to show that the freedom of agents is not merely a necessary condition for the moral worthiness of their actions and characters but also the sufficient condition or source of such value? It would be excessive generosity to claim that he has an explicit argument for this position in Section I of the *Groundwork*, but he may suggest at least a key premise of such an argument. We noted in our initial discussion of Kant's concept of the good will that the common fact that we evaluate actions and agents by their intended rather than actual outcomes does not by itself imply that the value of intending certain outcomes does not derive from the value those outcomes would have if they were realized, thus that this common fact about moral evaluation is compatible with the class of moral theories that are based on the value of certain outcomes (what are called consequentialist moral theories, of which traditional utilitarianism is the paradigmatic example). However, perhaps we can now see that Kant is not guilty of having failed to recognize this. For as we have seen, his analysis of duty has been based on the premise that there is no value in inclination as such. This implies not merely that performing an action freely rather than as it were mechanically from inclination alone is a necessary condition of the worthiness of that performance, but also that inclination cannot create value, certainly not unconditional value, in its own objects. Thus a theory that derives the value of consequences, and in turn of aiming at intended consequences, from the inclinations that make those objects for us cannot be a theory of unconditional value, and thus at least in Kant's view cannot be a genuine moral theory. So what is the alternative? Perhaps what Kant supposes, although this would need an argument he does not supply, is that the only alternative to inclination is free choice, so that free choice must itself be of unconditional value. This may be what he means when he says that if the worth of an action cannot derive from its aiming at an object of inclination, then the only alternative is that its worth derives solely from the '**principle of willing**' or the '**principle of the will** without regard to the ends that can be effected through such an action' (*G*, 4:400).

Kant would need more argument to reach this conclusion because there seems to be another alternative to the assumption that value comes from inclinations, namely that in addition to the contingent and at best conditionally valuable ends set by inclination there is another sort of an end that could be the source of unconditional value, namely a necessary end. We shall see that in Section II of the *Groundwork* Kant bases the obligatoriness of the categorical imperative that he reached at the end of Section I on the premise that adherence to this imperative is necessary to respect a necessary end, namely rational being or its human manifestation, what Kant calls in this context 'humanity,' as an end in itself. And we shall also see that by humanity Kant means nothing other than the ability to set our own particular ends freely rather than having them set for us by inclination. So Kant's arguments in Sections I and II may reach the same conclusion, namely that the only thing of unconditional value and therefore the only possible basis of a moral theory is free choice itself. Of course, a central question about Section II will then be whether Kant there has an argument for the unconditional value of humanity understood as the capacity for free choice other than the psychological argument for the value of freedom that he earlier used.

The central idea of Section II, the unconditional value of humanity as an end in itself, will then be what links the argument of the *Groundwork* to Kant's previous argument based explicitly on the premise that freedom is our unconditional end and reason and its rules merely the means to that end. But even in Section I, Kant plants a hint that he does not intend by this argument to dismiss completely the value of particular ends suggested to us by inclination. In a passage in his argument that reason must have a different end from producing happiness that might escape notice if the reader is not forearmed with knowledge of Kant's writings subsequent to the *Groundwork*, he writes:

> Yet since reason has been imparted to us as a practical faculty, i.e., one that should have an influence on the **will**, its true vocation must not be **as a means** to some other aim, but to produce **a will that is good in itself** . . . To be sure, this will need not be the sole and complete good, but it must be the highest good and the condition for all other goods, even the desire for happiness . . . (4:396)

Here Kant points toward a doctrine that he had already introduced in the *Critique of Pure Reason* (in the section entitled the 'Canon of Pure Reason') and that he would develop in detail in the *Critique of Practical Reason* and later writings,[16] the doctrine that the complete good for humankind consists in the maximum of virtue combined with the the maximum of happiness that is consistent with virtue, indeed as a product of virtue. Since happiness is nothing other than the sum of the gratification of particular inclinations, this doctrine presupposes the common-sense view that there is value in the gratification of inclinations and desires while preserving the Kantian point that there is no unconditional value in such gratification – the value of such gratification is rather conditional upon the prior satisfaction of the demands of morality. Still, to deny that the value of the gratification of inclinations is unconditional is not to deny that it is a value at all.

Kant will not explicitly develop his theory of the complete good further in the *Groundwork*. But as we will see in our discussion of Section II, he does introduce the key premise of this theory through his suggestion that establishing the 'realm of ends' requires not only respecting all human beings as ends in themselves but also in promoting their particular ends in a systematically coherent way, for the satisfaction of particular ends is what produces happiness. Thus we will see that while the concept of humanity as an end in itself is the fundamental premise of the philosophical argument of Section II, the concept of the realm of ends plays a key role in reconciling this philosophical argument with the common-sense morality to which Kant has appealed in Section I.

Study Questions

1. What is Kant's concept of the good will, and could it by itself lead to a particular conception of the fundamental principle of morality?
2. What is Kant's concept of duty, and could it by itself lead to a particular conception of the fundamental principle of morality?
3. What does Kant mean by moral worth, and why does he think that inclinations by themselves never have moral worth?
4. What are the proper roles of inclination in morally worthy action?

CHAPTER 5

READING THE TEXT: SECTION II.
FORMULATING THE CATEGORICAL IMPERATIVE

1. INTRODUCTION

In Section I of the *Groundwork* Kant derived the categorical imperative from common conceptions of good will and duty. His aim in
Section II is to derive it from sound philosophical premises in a way
that will *supplant* 'popular moral philosophy' but *be consistent with*
the 'common rational knowledge of morality' appealed to in Section
I. What will supplant popular moral philosophy is a 'metaphysics of
morals.' But now Kant uses this phrase in a way that is different from
his usage in the Preface to the *Groundwork*, where it meant all of the
pure rather than applied part of moral philosophy (what he there
called 'practical anthropology'), as well as from his usage in the later
Metaphysics of Morals, where the phrase instead means precisely the
applied part of moral philosophy. In Section II of the *Groundwork*,
'metaphysics of morals' designates the full *analysis* of the categorical imperative in what turn out to be its multiple formulations and
their derivation from key philosophical concepts. But the *proof* that
acting in accordance with this categorical imperative is both possible and necessary for we human beings is reserved for Section III,
where it will be based on what Kant calls both a 'critique of pure
practical reason' and a 'critique of the subject' (*G*, 4:440), or, we
might say, a critique of pure practical reason *in* the human subject.
Kant often emphasizes this division of labor by saying that the categorical imperative is a 'synthetic *a priori* proposition,' the *content*
of which can be discovered by analysis in Section II but our *cognition* of which can only be proven in Section III, although as we saw
in Chapter 3 this is not all that Kant means by saying that the
Groundwork uses both the analytical and the synthetic method. As

we saw there, Kant also calls the confirmation of the formulations of the categorical imperative that are derived by the analytical method from a classification of duties that are actually accepted a use of synthetic method. That confirmation is provided within Section II. So in discussing Section II, we have to ask both how Kant derives the categorical imperative in all its formulations and how well he succeeds in showing that it is congruent with common conceptions about human duties, if not in all their detail then at least in their general classes. Questions about whether he ultimately succeeds in proving the binding force of the categorical imperative for beings like us must be reserved for our discussion of Section III.

Kant supposes that 'popular moral philosophy' attempts to derive moral principles from empirical observation of actual human sentiments and conduct; in his view, such an approach can never give rise to genuinely necessary and universal principles, but conceptual analysis of the laws that a truly rational agent – a rational being with a will – would follow can. The central argument of Section II can thus be understood as an attempt to derive the several formulations of the categorical imperative from key features of the concept of a rational agent. Briefly, the argument is this: Unlike ordinary objects, which act in accordance with laws of nature but not with any consciousness of those laws, a rational agent is one that acts with and indeed from consciousness of the laws of its conduct. Further, while some laws of conduct are only means to certain particular ends, the force of which for particular agents depends upon whether they adopt those ends – these are what Kant calls 'hypothetical imperatives,' for their force depends upon the hypothesis that an agent has the relevant end – others can be recognized to be universally and necessary valid, or to apply categorically, without any conditions – in other words, categorical imperatives. But the only candidate for the status of categorical imperative is the imperative that Kant has already reached in Section I, namely the command to act only on maxims that could also be universal laws. Thus a rational agent seeking to act upon a universally and necessarily valid law would have to act in accordance with the principle of acting only on universalizable maxims. Next, Kant adds to the conception of a rational agent the supposition that such an agent would not act without some goal or object – an end – in mind, although that cannot be an end set by any inclination, or one the value of which is conditional upon the presence of such an inclination. The end that a fully rational agent has in mind must be something that is an end in itself, or an unconditional end. Kant will then claim that the only candidate for such an end is rational being itself, or, in the form in which we are acquainted with it, 'humanity,' and that the unconditional value of this end is the *ground* of any possible categorical imperative, that is, that the value of which justifies and necessitates adherence to the categorical imperative as already analyzed. Kant equates humanity with the ability to set one's own ends freely, a capacity that can be preserved in all agents only if each agent accepts the principle of acting only on maxims that everyone could freely agree to act upon, a condition that is certainly met by universalizable maxims. From these results, Kant will derive the further conclusion that a fully rational agent will act only upon maxims that recognize the freedom of all to determine the laws of their own conduct, that is, maxims that could be freely legislated by all for all. Borrowing a term from ancient political theory, Kant calls the condition of acting only on laws that one freely legislates for oneself 'autonomy,' but holds that the only such laws are those that everyone could freely legislate for everyone. Further, an autonomous agent in a community of autonomous agents each of whom fully respects the autonomy of all the others would not only act solely on maxims that recognize the right of all agents to determine their own particular ends freely, but would also promote the realization of those ends to the extent that this is possible and consistent with the universalizability of the maxims freely legislated by all. In other words, genuinely autonomous rational agents would also constitute a 'realm of ends,' a 'whole of all ends (of rational beings as ends in themselves as well as of the particular ends that each may set for himself)' (4:433). As Kant suggests, this result can also be reached by emphasizing the role of *systematicity* in the conception of rationality: a rational agent acts systematically, thus it necessarily aims for systematicity both in legislation and in the pursuit of particular ends. All of this, Kant supposes, can be derived from a proper analysis of the pure concept of a rational agent, and in that sense it is clearly an alternative to an empirically based 'popular moral philosophy.' But again, proving that *we* are in fact rational agents who both can and ought to achieve the goal of autonomy through adherence to the categorical imperative in these several formulations will await Section III of the *Groundwork*.

This argument will provide what was not clear in Section I, namely a connection between the categorical imperative and Kant's earlier argument that freedom is unconditionally valuable but can be preserved and promoted only through universal laws. For while Kant emphasizes that autonomy is the condition in which a rational agent gives law to itself, and thus that a community of autonomous agents is one in which each member can be considered to be a co-legislator of the laws by which the whole community abides, he also indicates that acting in accordance with laws that one gives to oneself is the only way in which one can avoid being determined by laws that come from outside oneself, whether from nature in general or from other persons considered merely as natural forces, and that *dignity* lies precisely in freeing oneself from determination by external forces, thus in autonomy. The *Groundwork*'s claim that dignity lies in freeing oneself from determination by nature by autonomously legislating laws for a realm of ends is its version of Kant's previous argument that the unconditional value of freedom can be realized only by acting in accordance with universal laws.

In the next section, we shall consider in more detail Kant's derivation of the formulations of the categorical imperative from the concept of a rational agent and his argument that only adherence to the categorical imperative yields autonomy – the 'analytical' phase of his argument in *Groundwork* II. In section 3, we will consider in closer detail whether Kant does establish that the value of autonomy is the basis of morality, and if so, how. In section 4, we will discuss that part of the 'synthetical' phase of Kant's argument that is included in *Groundwork* II, namely his attempt to confirm his analysis of the general principle of morality by showing that it gives rise to the commonly accepted classification of our actual moral duties and obligations. Thus, although Kant appeals to this classification twice in the course of his own exposition, after each of the first two of his main formulations of the categorical imperative, we shall postpone the full discussion of these examples until after we have laid out the main analytical argument of the whole Section. In section 5, we will examine Kant's distinction between 'perfect' and 'imperfect' duties, an important part of his classification of duties that bears on the application of the categorical imperative. In section 6, finally, we will consider some of the most common objections to the categorical imperative.

2. FROM THE CONCEPT OF A RATIONAL AGENT TO THE FORMULAE OF THE CATEGORICAL IMPERATIVE

i. Kant's Critique of 'Popular Moral Philosophy'

Section II of the *Groundwork* begins with several pages of criticism of 'popular moral philosophy' (4:406–10). Here Kant actually says more than just that no attempt at a moral theory grounded on empirical observation can yield genuinely necessary and universal moral principles, and more than that attempting to base moral principles on actual examples of human behavior will give rise to a theory that actually privileges self-love; he also argues that recognizing any actions as attempts at moral conduct at all, whether imperfect or perfect, *presupposes* that we have an antecedent and independent conception of the moral principles of which such conduct is supposed to be an example. This is part of Kant's argument that the fundamental principle of morality can only be known by *a priori* analysis.

Kant starts his argument by insisting that his own derivation of the characteristics of duty from the 'common use of our practical reason' in Section I of the *Groundwork* should not be interpreted as a reduction of the concept of duty to an 'empirical concept' (*Erfahrungsbegriff*) (4:406); this is why his illustrations of action from duty there should be understood as thought-experiments, not empirical descriptions. If one were to try to derive moral principles from empirical observation of actual human conduct, one would probably end up with a moral principle advocating 'more or less refined self-love,' because a vast number of human actions, even when they are in outward conformity with the demands of duty, are actually motivated by self-love, or at least, since self-love is so good at disguising itself, we cannot exclude even by the 'most rigorous scrutiny' that outwardly dutiful actions have been motivated by 'secret incentives.' Thus 'It is in fact absolutely impossible to make out from experience with complete certainty even a single case where the maxim of an otherwise dutiful action has rested solely on moral grounds and on the representation of one's duty' (4:407). However, Kant does not infer from this apparently pessimistic assessment of actual human conduct that it will be impossible to formulate any moral principle other than that of self-love; on the contrary, he argues that our recognition of the imperfection of so much of our knowledge of actual motivation and our recognition of the imperfection of so much actual human conduct both presuppose that we actually know what morally correct and worthy conduct would be. Thus he observes that the very fact that so many philosophers in all ages 'have mentioned with inner regret the fragility and impurity of human nature' has not led them 'to bring the correctness of the concept of morality into doubt,' but rather presupposes their recognition of the 'respect-worthy idea' of morality (4:406). Kant's point is that it is only in light of our knowledge of the idea of morality and its fundamental principle, even if that knowledge is only tacit, that we can recognize that so many actual examples of human conduct are imperfect and human character is so often frail and impure; if we did not have that independent standard by which to evaluate actual human conduct and character, we would have no reason to regard it as flawed or in any way short of ideal. Without knowledge of an ideal, you cannot recognize anything as less than ideal.

Even if there were a perfect moral agent, Kant next argues, our recognition of its moral perfection would presuppose that we have antecedent and independent knowledge of the moral principle that it perfectly exemplifies. Thus we cannot derive our conception of what is right and wrong from purported revelations of the commands of the divine will, but could only recognize such commands *as* manifestations of the divine will if we have an antecedent knowledge of what is right and holy (4:408). Thus, recognizing either an imperfect example or even a perfect example as an example of moral conduct presupposes that we have an antecedent concept of morality, so our knowledge of the fundamental principle of morality can only be *a priori*. The problem with an empirical method for the discovery of moral principles is thus not merely that it leads to an inadequate or erroneous moral principle; it is actually methodologically incoherent.

Before we turn to the positive argument that occupies the bulk of Section II, namely the derivation of the formulae of the categorical imperative from the very idea of a rational agent, we might note one other point that Kant makes in his critique of 'popular moral philosophy.' This is that any 'mixed doctrine of morals, which is put together from incentives of feeling and inclinations and at the same time concepts of reason, must leave the mind wavering between motives that cannot be brought under any principle, and thus can only quite contingently lead to the good, but often also to evil,' while the 'pure representation of duty . . . and of the moral law in general has through reason alone . . . such an influence on the human heart so much more powerful than all other incentives that may be offered from the empirical field that in the consciousness of its dignity it despises the latter and gradually becomes their master' (4:410–11). The natural way to read this passage (previously cited in our discussion of the feeling of respect) might seem to be that it would first require a demonstration of the existence of a pure moral principle before that principle could have its powerful effect on the human heart; but perhaps Kant is suggesting that we do feel the powerful influence of the moral law on our hearts even without having encountered any indubitable examples of moral conduct in our experience, and thus have another piece of evidence for our recognition of the moral law antecedent to any conclusive examples of actually moral conduct.

Whether or not this last point is persuasive, it is clear that Kant has meant his critique of any attempt to ground moral philosophy empirically to prepare the way for his own argument that its principle must be *a priori*. Kant also expresses this demand by saying that the moral law 'must be valid not merely for human beings, but for all *rational beings in general*, not merely under contingent conditions and with exceptions, but *absolutely necessarily*' (4:408). In order to satisfy this demand, the moral law and its various formulations will have to be derived from the concept of a rational being in general rather than from any empirical knowledge of human nature. But this is not to say that Kant's argument will presuppose that there *are* any rational beings other than human beings. His demand that the principle of morality be valid for all rational beings and be derivable from a general concept of rational beings is another way of saying it must be *a priori*, and so must be derivable from something in us that is pure and could be shared with other rational beings if there are any – namely, our reason rather than our inclinations. At the same time, it will be crucial to Kant's account of why the fundamental principle of morality presents itself to us as a categorical *imperative* that we ourselves are *not* purely rational beings and do have inclinations that arise from sense rather than from reason. Indeed, Kant will not only argue that we have sensible inclinations that can be a source of resistance to the moral law and thus make it seem like an imperative to us; it will also be at least a tacit part of his theory that we actually need sensible inclinations to suggest particular goals of action to us, and thus to allow us to be not merely rational *beings* but rational *agents*, insofar as we can be rational.

ii. Rational Agency and Universal Law

The philosophical derivation of the categorical imperative in Section II, then, begins from the premise that 'since moral laws should be valid for every rational being in general, they are to be derived from the universal concept of a rational being.' From this starting-point, Kant says, 'we must follow and clearly exhibit the practical faculty of reason from its universal rules of determination to the point where the concept of duty arises from it' (4:412). By this Kant does not mean that the *Groundwork* will derive all our particular duties from the general principle of morality; that task will be reserved for the later *Metaphysics of Morals*, although the *Groundwork* will show how certain key *examples* of particular duties can be derived from its formulations of the moral law in order to confirm the correctness of its analysis of the latter. Rather, what Kant means by this reference to the *concept* of duty is that he will show how the fundamental principle of morality that is to be derived from the universal concept of a rational being in general turns into an *imperative* when applied to the kind of rational beings that we human beings are, namely, rational beings who also have inclinations that can come into conflict with the requirements of morality.

The argument begins with the observation that while 'every thing in nature operates in accordance with laws,' 'Only a rational being has the capacity to act **in accordance with the representation** of laws, i.e., in accordance with principles, or a **will**.' Although this may not be a complete characterization of all the conditions necessary for an agent to count as rational, it is at least a necessary condition of rationality that an agent be conscious of the laws in accordance with which it acts and that it act as it does because it takes those laws to be reasons for so acting, or principles. By contrast, the law of gravitational attraction in accordance with which a falling body acts is not anything of which the falling body is aware, unless the falling body unfortunately happens to be a physicist, nor is this law a reason or principle for a falling body, even for the unfortunate physicist. Kant's next statement is one that can cause all sorts of problems if taken out of context: he says that 'Since for the derivation of actions from laws **reason** is required, thus the will is nothing other than practical reason' (4:412). Considered by itself, this is a *non sequitur*: what

Kant has previously said is that being able to act in conscious accord with a principle is a *necessary* condition for being a rational agent capable of rational willing; he has not said that it is a *sufficient condition*, which is what the present statement implies. However, the remainder of the paragraph makes it clear that Kant does *not* mean to say that in the case of human beings the will is identical to practical reason, for he goes on to say that while for a rational being for whom 'reason determined the will without exception' the will would be 'a capacity to choose **only that** which reason, independent from inclination, recognized as practically necessary, i.e., as good,' and thus for such a being the will would be identical with practical reason, *the human being is not that sort of rational being*. In human beings, reason does not automatically determine the will by itself, for human beings 'are subject to subjective conditions (certain incentives) that do not always correspond to objective' ones, i.e., to the demands of reason, and so the human 'will is not **in itself** completely in harmony with reason.' Rather, for human beings 'the actions that are recognized as objectively necessary are subjectively contingent, and the determination of such a will according to objective laws is **necessitation**.' Thus, the principles of practical reason in accordance with which a *human* will is aware that it must act present themselves to it as imperatives that are not necessarily in accord with all of its inclinations and desires: 'The representation of an objective principle insofar as it is necessitating for a will is called a **command** (of reason) and the formula of the command is called an **imperative**' (4:412–13). That the objective principles of reason present themselves to us as imperatives is a sign of our incomplete rationality, which is to say that for us the will is *not* simply identical to practical reason.

Now one might think that this analysis is supposed to apply only to the moral demands of *pure* practical reason, that is, that Kant is saying that we imperfect human beings sometimes find the demands of morality to be a constraint upon our inclinations but that we do not find other demands of practical rationality to be constraints. However, the classification of imperatives that Kant now expounds reveals that we are so imperfectly rational that we can find *any* principle of practical reason to be a constraint and thus an imperative, even when morality is not at issue. For there are two main types of principles of practical reason, or, since the first type contains two subtypes, three types of such principles, and all of them can present themselves to us as constraints upon our inclinations. The two main types of imperatives are what Kant calls *hypothetical* and *categorical* imperatives. Hypothetical imperatives 'represent the practical necessity of a possible action as a means to attain something else that one wills (or that it is possible that one would will).' These imperatives are called 'hypothetical' because they apply to particular agents only subject to the hypothesis that they do or may want the end to which acting in accordance with these rules is the means; in other words, they apply only conditionally, that is, subject to the condition that one does or may have that end. By contrast, 'the categorical imperative would be that which represents an object as objectively necessary for itself, without relation to another end.' Similarly, Kant says that if an action is 'good merely **for something else**, as a means, then the imperative is **hypothetical**,' but 'if it is represented as good **in itself**, hence as necessary as the principle of a will that is in itself in harmony with reason, then it is **categorical**' (4:414). These characterizations are often taken, indeed by Kant himself, to mean that while a hypothetical imperative represents some particular action as necessary as a means to some particular end, a categorical imperative does not represent the actions that it commands as means to any end at all, but as good entirely in themselves. However, the contrast between conditional and absolute validity, subjective and objective validity, or validity merely for some agents and validity for all possible agents that underlies Kant's contrast between merely hypothetical and genuinely categorical imperatives neither requires nor entails such a conclusion. What it requires is only a distinction between *contingent* ends and *necessary* ends: if a principle tells one how to realize a contingent end, then it would apply to and be binding for one only if one happens to have that end, while if a principle tells one how to realize a *necessary* end, an end that one must have, then it applies to one regardless of any particular ends one happens to have, or categorically. And in fact Kant will subsequently argue that the possibility of the categorical imperative *depends* upon the discovery of a necessary end, namely rational being or humanity as an end in itself. The structure of Kant's entire argument in *Groundwork* II would thus be undermined if a categorical imperative really had no relation to any kind of end at all. Kant can only mean that the validity of the categorical imperative for every agent does not depend upon any *contingent* end, set by mere inclination.

This point might be obscured by Kant's next step, the division of hypothetical imperatives into two types, which leads to his ultimate trifold division of imperatives. Hypothetical imperatives are divided into 'imperatives of **skill**' (4:415), also called 'technical' imperatives (4:416), which prescribe rules to particular ends that one might or might not happen to have (and for that reason are further called '**problematic**' imperatives at 4:415), and imperatives prescribing rules for one end that it can be presumed that everyone *does* have – for this reason this kind of hypothetical imperative can be called '**assertoric**,' that is, stating a fact (4:415). This one end that everyone does have is nothing other than happiness, and for that reason this sort of hypothetical imperative is also called an imperative of '**prudence**' (4:416) or a '**pragmatic**' imperative for 'welfare' (4:417). The reason why this distinction might obscure the point made in the previous paragraph is that Kant treats happiness as an end that *everyone* has, which might make happiness sound like a necessary end. Indeed, if one supposes that everyone has the end of happiness because of a law of nature, it might even sound like a naturally necessary end. But Kant's claim is that from the point of view of all rational beings, not just natural human beings, it is still a contingent end. More convincingly, perhaps, what he goes on to argue is that in a way the singleness of the end of happiness for all human beings is illusory, because different people (or even the same person at different times) place their happiness in different things or different goals (4:416). One person would be made happy, or thinks he would be, by achieving wealth and fame for a wide public, while another might be made happy by a frugal life of intellectual accomplishment appreciated only by a few. 'Happiness' is just a name for the satisfaction of desires that can be quite different and indeed incommensurable from one person to another. Thus, imperatives of skill can be quite definite, even though the ends the necessary means to which they prescribe are contingent – the precepts that are necessary for the doctor in order to make his patient healthy and those that are necessary for the poisoner in order to be sure of killing his victim are equally definite, even though obviously not everyone shares those ends – but since not everyone defines his own happiness in the same way, and indeed since people are often quite unclear about what would really make even themselves happy in the long run, there can be no very definite imperatives for reaching happiness. When it comes to happiness there are only 'empirical counsels' or advice, 'e.g., of diet, frugality, courtesy, restraint, etc.,' which will perhaps help many people achieve happiness much of the time, but which cannot be guaranteed to be means to happiness always and for everybody. 'The imperatives of prudence cannot command, i.e., exhibit actions objectively as practically-**necessary**, but . . . are to be taken as advice (*consilia*) rather than as commands (*praecepta*) of reason' (4:417). Thus, although there might seem to be an important difference between the imperatives of skill and the imperatives of prudence for the sake of happiness, in fact both of them prescribe means that are necessary only for contingent and variable ends, while the categorical imperative need not prescribe actions without relation to any ends at all, but can apply to all agents unconditionally as long as it turns out to prescribe the only means to a genuinely necessary end.

That is how Kant will ultimately present the categorical imperative, but there will be several steps in his argument before he gets there. Before we continue with that argument, however, let us return to a point mentioned a moment ago, namely that *any* principle of reason can present itself to us as a constraint, not just the universally valid principle of morality that presents itself to us as the categorical imperative. Why is this so? That is, how can a principle that tells us what steps it is necessary to take in order to achieve some merely arbitrary end, whether that end is considered in isolation as in the case of an imperative of skill or as part of our overall happiness as in the case of a counsel of prudence, be considered to be a constraint? How can such a principle be a constraint if the end to which it prescribes the means is contingent and could therefore be given up? The answer to this question is that even when it comes to contingent or arbitrary ends we humans are not perfectly rational beings: thus, we could very much want to be slim or rich, know perfectly well that the only way to become slim is through diet and exercise and the only to become rich is through hard work and disciplined investment, and still want to laze around eating and spending self-indulgently. Thus, even though the imperatives of skill and prudence do not exhibit principles of *pure* practical reason, just of ordinary practical reason, they can still seem like constraints to us.

This point needs to be kept in mind as we now consider the next step in Kant's argument, leading up to the first formulation of the categorical imperative in the second section of the *Groundwork*.

After having laid out his distinction among technical imperatives and pragmatic imperatives as the two varieties of hypothetical imperatives and the moral imperative as the sole categorical imperative (4:416–17), Kant asks 'How are all these imperatives possible?', meaning to ask by this not 'how the execution of the action that the imperative commands' is possible but 'merely how the necessitation of the will that is the task that the imperative expresses can be conceived' (4:417). In other words, his question is what makes an imperative binding or obligatory for us? He says that there is really no problem about why hypothetical imperatives are binding, because the principle that 'Whoever wills the end wills (insofar as reason has a decisive influence on his actions) the means' is analytic, that is, what it means genuinely to will some end is to be prepared and willing to take sufficient steps to achieve that goal, while to be unwilling to take such steps means that one does not really will the end after all. This would be true if we were fully rational, although as has just been pointed out even these principles are imperatives precisely because we are not always completely rational – a point that Kant himself makes when he says that the principle that 'whoever wills the ends will the means' is analytic only insofar as reason does in fact have a 'decisive influence' on us. Kant claims that this principle self-evidently explains the possibility of imperatives of skill, that is, in those cases it is quite obvious to us that insofar as we are to be rational we will have to give up the ends if we do not like the means, or reconcile ourselves to the means if we are not prepared to give up the ends. The implications of the principle may be less obvious in the case of happiness, where it may not be so clear that taking steps to preserve our health, for example, will really lead to happiness, because if one 'wills a long life, who will guarantee him that it will not be a long misery,' or if one saves scrupulously for one's old age, who will guarantee that one will not die prematurely, leaving all the money to some worthless heir? (4:418) But here the problem is just that both our conceptions of happiness and of the means to it are 'indeterminate' and 'empirical': that is, although in a general way of course we all want happiness, we do not really know precisely what particular things would make us happy, and in any case general advice on how to get such things is always vague and imperfect. But if we did know precisely what would make us happy and if the means to achieving whatever exactly would constitute happiness on that assumption were completely clear, then the principle 'whoever wills the end wills the means' would also apply: as Kant puts it, the 'imperative of prudence would be an analytical-practical proposition if one assumed that' both the constituents and 'the means to happiness could be specified' precisely (4:419).

The possibility of hypothetical imperatives is therefore explained by the fact that they simply express the necessary means to particular ends that we have adopted, even if our imperfect rationality means that this fact is not sufficient to guarantee that such imperatives will always have a 'decisive influence' on our actions. Kant then says that

> By contrast, how the imperative of **morality** is possible is without doubt the only question that is in need of a solution, since it is not hypothetical at all and therefore cannot support its objectively-represented necessity on any presupposition, as in the case of the hypothetical imperatives. (4:419)

What he seems to mean by this is that the possibility of the categorical imperative of morality cannot be explained by the principle 'Whoever wills the end wills the means' because the validity of the categorical imperative does not depend upon the presupposition of any end at all. However, when Kant further explains the problem of the possibility of the categorical imperative by using his preferred terminology of synthetic *a priori* propositions, saying that insight into the possibility of the categorical imperative is very difficult because it is a 'synthetical-practical proposition *a priori*,' and explains this in turn by saying that through the categorical imperative

> I connect the deed with the will *a priori*, without a presupposed condition from any inclination (although objectively, i.e., under the idea of a reason that would have complete power over all subjective motivations). It is therefore a practical proposition, which does not derive the willing of an action analytically from another one that is already presupposed (for we have no such perfect will), but rather connects it immediately with the concept of the will as of a rational being as something that is not contained in it, (4:420n)

he suggests instead that the binding force of the categorical imperative upon us cannot be explained by our adoption of any *contingent* end. Since the categorical imperative does not command actions as means to ends set by inclination, its possibility cannot be explained by the fact that we have such inclinations and the ends associated with them combined with the analytical principle that whoever wills the ends wills the means. That is Kant's explicit reason for stating here that the categorical imperative must be synthetic. And since he has been asserting from the beginning of the *Groundwork* that the fundamental principle of morality must be *a priori*, he now infers that if it is synthetic then it must also be synthetic *a priori*, and therefore explaining its possibility will be as difficult as explaining the possibility of synthetic *a priori* propositions in theoretical philosophy, which of course was the central task of the *Critique of Pure Reason*. Yet at the same time Kant wants to warn us that the fact that the categorical imperative is synthetic *a priori* and thus in some sense connects an action that it prescribes with the will *a priori* does not mean that *human* beings automatically do what the categorical imperative prescribes. The categorical imperative connects the deed synthetically yet immediately with the concept of a purely rational will, but Kant reminds us that *we* do not have such a perfect will.

Kant thus sets up the challenge for explaining the possibility of the categorical imperative by saying that it immediately connects morally requisite actions with the idea of a rational will – although it does not connect them automatically with the actual human will – without characterizing those actions as means to any end of inclination. However, Kant also says that while we can always escape from the constraint of some hypothetical imperative by simply 'giving up the goal,' which we can do if the goal is merely an arbitrary one suggested by inclination, 'by contrast the unconditional command' of the categorical imperative 'leaves the will no choice with regard to its opposite' (4:420) because the validity of the categorical imperative does not depend upon its prescribing the means to any end at all. There is here the same gap in Kant's argumentation, indeed conflict with the real structure of his overall argument, that we found in his derivation of the categorical imperative in Section I of the *Groundwork*: although if it is to be *a priori* the categorical imperative clearly cannot prescribe morally necessary actions as means to merely contingent ends set by inclination, this does not imply that it cannot prescribe actions as means to any end at all; the possibility remains open that it can prescribe actions as necessary means to a necessary end. Indeed, introducing a necessary end and showing how adherence to the categorical imperative is the necessary means to this end will subsequently become the key step in Kant's answer to the question of how the categorical imperative is possible: that the categorical imperative prescribes the necessary means to a necessary end is what makes it obligatory for us to adhere to it.

Kant does not make this clear immediately, because he now says that his next step will be to see whether 'the mere concept of a categorical imperative also provides the formula that contains the proposition that can alone be a categorical imperative,' while further consideration of the question 'how such an absolute command is possible' can be deferred until the third section of the *Groundwork* (4:420). This is misleading, because the issue in Section III will be that of showing that the categorical imperative is possible for the *human* will, specifically that the human will is both obligated by it and also capable of fulfilling it, while Kant's further moves in Section II will show how the categorical imperative is possible for a *purely rational* will by introducing the necessary end that is immediately connected to the idea of such a will and to which adherence to the categorical imperative is the only possible means. And this also means that we must handle Kant's claim that the categorical imperative is a synthetic *a priori* practical proposition carefully: this further step in the explanation of the possibility of the categorical imperative will be synthetic insofar as it requires going beyond the *present conception* of a rational will merely as one that acts in accordance with its own representation of a law to a fuller conception of a rational will as one that acts for the sake of a necessary end; but this fuller conception of a rational will will still be a *concept* of a rational will, and to that extent Kant's further argument in *Groundwork* II will still proceed by analysis even if it yields a synthetic conclusion, with the proof of the *further* synthetic proposition that this conclusion applies to *us* being left to *Groundwork* III.

With this warning in mind, let us return to the progress of Kant's argument where we left it. Kant said that he would try to derive the formula of the categorical imperative from the mere concept of such an imperative. What he now claims is that since the concept of a categorical imperative is that of an imperative that is valid independent of any condition, 'there remains nothing with which the maxim of an action is to be in accord except for the universality of a law in general, which accordance alone the imperative really represents as necessary' (4:421). In other words, since a categorical imperative by definition cannot prescribe an action or more accurately a maxim of action as a means to a contingent end and Kant has not yet introduced the idea of it as prescribing a maxim as the necessary means to a necessary end, all it can do is prescribe that maxims themselves be categorical, that is, be possible as universal laws. Thus Kant derives the first formulation of the categorical imperative in *Groundwork* II, essentially identical to the formulation derived from the common conception of duty in Section I: '**Act only in accordance with such a maxim through which you can at the same time will that it become a universal law.**' We will henceforth call this the Formula of Universal Law (FUL).

Kant says that while he will continue to leave unsettled the question of whether duty is an 'empty concept,' that is, whether this principle actually can and does constrain us (for that is what 'duty' means), he will demonstrate that from this one general imperative all particular imperatives of duty can be derived. He will attempt to do this by showing how a representative duty from each of the commonly recognized main classes of duty can be derived from this general principle. But even before he attempts to do this, he reformulates the principle by saying that since the idea of 'nature in the most general sense (as far as form is concerned)' is nothing but the idea of a domain of objects that is determined in accordance with universal laws, the idea of a domain of agents universally accepting or following the maxim on which one proposes to act is equivalent to the idea of a domain in which that maxim has become a law of nature; thus the categorical imperative can also be formulated as the imperative to '**act as if the maxim of your action were to become through your will a *universal law of nature*'** (4:421). This version of the principle is known as the Formula of the Law of Nature (FLN). Some interpreters, encouraged by the first of Kant's following examples of the application of the categorical imperative for the derivation of particular duties, in which he argues that suicide to avoid further suffering out of the motive of self-love is contrary to the idea of a law of nature which always uses a single cause for a single effect, namely self-love for the prolongation of life (4:422), have argued that FLN makes a significant addition to FUL by introducing a teleological conception of nature, like the one to which Kant appealed in his discussion of the true function of reason in Section I (4:395–6), in which each natural organ or capacity has only

may still be a problem about how to identify the particular maxim on which an agent is actually proposing to act and to which the categorical imperative is to be applied, for it might turn out that the very same action is permissible if its maxim is described one way but not if it is described another way. But for now let us just get a general idea of how Kant proposes to apply FUL/FLN. After he has stated these two formulae of the categorical imperative, Kant considers four examples of general classes of duty according to what is supposed to be a common and exhaustive classification of duties. We can leave the details of that classification for later. We can also skip Kant's first example for the time being, the example of suicide, since we have already seen that it is problematic. So let us consider Kant's second example. This is the example of someone considering getting out of a financial scrape by promising to repay a loan even though he has no intention of doing so. He is proposing to act on the maxim 'If I believe myself to be in financial need I will borrow money and promise to pay it back [in order to get out of my difficulty] although I also know that this will never happen.' He is then supposed to ask 'How it would stand if my maxim were a universal law,' that is, to consider whether this maxim is consistent with FUL/FLN, that is, whether he could act upon it if everyone else were to do so as well. He then is supposed to see right away 'that it could never be valid as a universal law of nature and agree with itself, rather that it must necessarily contradict itself,'

> For the universality of a law that everyone who believes himself to be in need could promise whatever occurs to him with the intention of not keeping his promise would make the promise itself and the end that one may have in it impossible, for nobody would believe what was promised to him, but would laugh at such an utterance as an idle pretense. (4:422)

That is, in a world in which everyone made false promises – and remember, as we saw in the previous chapter, Kant is not saying that such a world would actually result from one person making one or even many false promises, but is rather asking us to perform the thought-experiment of considering what would be possible *if* such a world existed – would be one in which no one in his right mind would accept a promise, and thus one's own plan of getting out of trouble by making a false promise would become impossible. That is, because a world of false promises is actually logically impossible, there would be a practical contradiction between one's own maxim of making a false promise and the universalization of that maxim: you could not will the universalization of the maxim and still successfully act upon the maxim.[4] Thus, such a maxim would violate FUL/FLN and be impermissible, while its converse, namely something like 'In similar circumstances make only promises that you sincerely intend to keep,' would be morally mandatory. (Again, the impermissibility of false promises in order to get out of financial trouble does not imply that false promises are impermissible in *all* circumstances.)

Or take Kant's fourth example. This is the example of someone for whom things are going well and who proposes to adopt toward others for whom things are going less well and could benefit from his help the maxim 'Let each be as happy as heaven wills or as he can make himself, I will take nothing away from him, indeed not even envy him; only I have no pleasure to contribute something to his well-being or to his assistance in time of need' (4:423), that is, something like 'In a world in which others are in need of my help, in order to continue enjoying my own good fortune I will not help them.' Here Kant argues that although there is no logical contradiction in imagining such a world – others around one could go to rack and ruin and yet one might still enjoy one's own good fortune – yet there is nevertheless a practical contradiction between one's maxim and its universalization, because one ought to realize that one's own good fortune might not last forever, thus that there might be situations in which one would indeed need the help of others, but that by willing the universalization of one's own maxim, that is, willing that *no one* who is enjoying good fortune help others who are not, one would have deprived oneself of the help that one would then need, thus of the means to one's own renewed good fortune. In Kant's words, 'A will that resolved upon this' universalization of a maxim of indifference to the needs of others 'would contradict itself because cases could easily arise in which it needed the love and sympathy of others but where, through such a law of nature sprung from its own will, it would have robbed itself of all help of the assistance that it wishes.' That is, a rational will does not just consider its immediate circumstances, but its possible future circumstances as well, and does not adopt maxims the universalization of which would undermine its own will, such as the will to enjoy well-being and good fortune, in those possible circumstances. Thus the maxim of indifference to others in need is impermissible, and one must instead adopt the converse of this maxim, namely, the principle to help at least some others in some circumstances of their need.

Again, there are many issues about these and Kant's other examples that need to be discussed in more detail. But let us leave those questions aside for now, and grant that Kant has established that the concept of acting only on universalizable maxims does give rise to particular duties in a straightforward way. This could be taken to be the fulfillment of the first stage of Kant's analysis of the concept of a rational will: a being that acts only in accordance with maxims that it can also represent as universal laws will in fact recognize that it has certain duties. But now the question arises of whether this is a sufficient conception of rational willing. Why should a rational being act only in accordance with universal laws if there is *no* end to be achieved thereby, as Kant's exposition to this point sometimes seems to suggest? After all, it also seems to be part of our conception of rationality that a rational agent acts on certain principles only in order to attain certain goals. Yet of course Kant has insisted that acting for the sake of merely contingent or arbitrary goals set by inclination is inconsistent with the universal and necessary demands of morality. Acting for the sake of such goals cannot be what makes accepting the constraint of the categorical imperative rational. So what does? Here is the point where, in spite of his previous language suggesting that the moral law depends on no relation to any ends at all, Kant clearly introduces the idea of an objective and necessary rather than subjective and contingent end as that which makes the categorical imperative rational.

iii. The rational will and an unconditional end

The next part of Section II (4:425–31) is crucial, because here Kant makes clear that the reason for any agent to adhere to the categorical imperative as thus far formulated (that is, FUL/FLN) is the fact that such adherence is the necessary means to an end, but an objective and necessary rather than subjective and contingent end, namely rational being in general and humanity in our case. But it is also frustrating, because Kant does not explicitly define this end nor does he offer a clear argument for its status as a necessary end. Our task now must be to see whether we can throw additional light on these issues.

Kant begins this passage by claiming that by his exposition of FUL and FLN he has 'exhibited the content of the categorical imperative, which would have to contain the principle of all duty (if there is in general such a thing) clearly and determined for every use,' but has 'not gotten as far as proving *a priori* that such an imperative really obtains,' and he then reiterates that the proof of the validity of the categorical imperative cannot rest on anything empirical, or on any '**particular characteristic of human nature**.' Likewise the proof cannot depend upon any 'implanted sense or who knows what whispered by a guardian nature' (4:425), another slap at moral sense and divine command ethical theories. The principle of moral action must be 'free of all experiences of contingent grounds that only experience can provide' (4:426). In order to determine whether it is in fact 'a necessary law **for all rational beings** always to judge their actions in accordance with such maxims that they themselves could will to serve as universal laws,' that is, to discover whether what has thus far been formulated in the form of FUL and FLN is really binding on all rational beings, Kant says that we must take a 'further step' into the metaphysics of morals. What he has in mind by this phrase here is that we must further analyze the concept of a rational agent. Thus far, we have analyzed this concept only as the concept of a being that acts in accordance with its own conscious representation of laws rather than merely in unwitting conformity with laws, like a falling stone. Now Kant says that the will of a rational agent is not merely a capacity 'to determine itself to action **in accordance with the representation of certain laws**,' but also that a rational will determines itself to act in accordance with laws on the basis of an end, to which conformity to those laws is the means: 'Now that which serves the will as the objective ground of its self-determination is the **end**' (4:427). Kant's assumption, and it is a very natural one, is that to choose to adhere to a law without any goal to be achieved by so doing would not be the model of rationality but rather the height of irrationality; so if rational beings are to conform themselves to the fundamental principle of morality rationally, they must have a goal in so doing. But we know that this goal cannot be anything subjective and contingent like the satisfaction of a mere inclination; rather, if the end 'is to be given through mere reason, it must be equally valid for all rational beings.' The validity of the moral law for all rational beings cannot rest on merely 'subjective grounds of desire,' or '**incentives**' (*Triebfedern*), and the 'subjective ends' that they suggest, but must rest on 'objective' grounds of desire, or '**motives** [*Bewegungsgründe*] that are valid for every rational being.' And here Kant introduces an important clarification: to insist that the fundamental principle of morality must be 'formal,' as he does, does not mean that it must involve no relation to any end whatsoever; it means only that it must 'abstract from all subjective ends,' which are what would make it '**material**' and 'relative' and would make all imperatives merely hypothetical, valid only for a 'faculty of desire of a subject constituted in a particular way' (4:428). Thus Kant can now say that in order for there to be a valid categorical imperative 'there would have to be something **the existence of which has an absolute value in itself**, which, as an **end in itself**, could be a ground of determinate laws,' and that only in such an end 'would the ground of a possible categorical imperative, i.e., of practical laws, lie.' In other words, Kant's conception of rational agency preserves the means-end structure characteristic of the ordinary conception of rationality, where adoption of a rule makes sense only if it is the means to an end; his addition to this ordinary analysis is just that if rules are to be universal and necessary, then they must be the necessary means to a necessary end, something that is necessarily an end because it is not itself the means to some further end of arbitrary value, but is itself intrinsically and absolutely valuable.

The next question, of course, is what could such an end be, and here Kant's patient analysis suddenly gives way to bald assertion. Kant bluntly proceeds: 'Now I say: the human being and in general every rational being **exists** as an end in itself, **not merely as a means** for the arbitrary use of this or some other will, but must in all of its actions directed toward rational beings, both toward itself and toward others, always be considered **at the same time as an end**' (4:428). Kant explicates this assertion by saying that 'objects of inclination have only a conditional value,' but that the 'inclinations themselves, as sources of needs, are so far from having any absolute value that the wish to be entirely free of them would rather be the universal wish of every rational being.' This is clearly an overstatement, for if no rational being had any inclinations creating any needs, then there would be nothing for any rational being *to do*, whether for himself or for any other rational being, and thus rational beings could not be rational *agents*. The picture that Kant properly suggests elsewhere in his writings, including elsewhere in the *Groundwork*, is that the ends suggested by inclination have merely conditional value and it is the universal wish of every rational being to *regulate* those ends by subordinating them to a principle grounded in an end of unconditional or absolute value; thus, as he more accurately says a few pages later, 'the principle of humanity and of every rational nature in general **as an end in itself**' is the 'supreme limiting condition on the freedom of the actions of every human being' in the pursuit of particular ends of merely conditional value (4:430–1). Kant continues the present exposition by also stating that 'beings without reason have only a relative value, as means, and are thus called **things**,' fully available to us for our own use without any constraints arising from their own character. 'By contrast, rational beings are called **persons**, because their nature already distinguishes them as ends in themselves, i.e., as something that may not be used merely as a means, hence as something that restricts all choice (and is an object of respect)' (4:428). By means of these considerations, Kant reaches his second main formulation of the categorical imperative (or third, if one wants to distinguish FLN from FUL): '**Act so that you always use humanity, both in your own person as well as in that of every other, at the same time as an end and never merely as a means**' (4:429). This can be called the Formula of the End in Itself (FEI).

Kant's comments leading up to FEI tell us a little about what it is *not* to treat a being as an end in itself, but do not tell us very much positive about what it *is* to treat someone as an end in itself. Nor do they suggest any argument underlying Kant's bald 'Now I say.' The paragraph immediately preceding Kant's bold-letter statement of FEI might seem to address at least the second of these issues by offering an argument for FEI. Here Kant first reiterates the appeal to means-end reasoning on which this whole stage of his analysis is based:

> If, then, there is to be a supreme practical principle and, with regard to the human will, a categorical imperative, then it must be one that from the representation of that which is necessarily an end for everyone because it is **an end in itself** constitutes an **objective** principle of the will, hence can serve as a practical law.

He then states what might seem like an argument for FEI:

> The ground of this principle is: **rational nature exists as an end in itself**. The human being necessarily represents his own existence thus; to this extent it is a **subjective** principle of human actions.

But every other rational being also represents his own existence, consequently the very same rational ground that is also valid for me, this way; thus it is at the same time an **objective** principle from which, as a supreme practical principle, all laws of the will must be able to be derived. (4:428–9)

And then Kant says that 'the practical imperative will therefore be' FEI.

But this cannot be an argument that because each of us represents *his or her own* existence as an end in itself, 'subjectively' or for his or her self, therefore the existence of *each* of us is an end in itself for *all* of us. An objective conclusion like that cannot follow from a merely subjective premise; that would be like inferring that because each of us loves his or her own spouse, all of us must love everyone else's spouses. Rather, Kant must be saying that in fact each of us subjectively regards his or her own existence as an end in itself because we all already accept the *objective* principle that every rational being is an end in itself and then apply that principle to our own case. But if that is the proper logical structure of Kant's argument here, then it does not further explain or justify his initial bald assertion that every human being and in general every rational being is an end in itself; rather, it presupposes it. It would seem that Kant still owes us an argument for this assertion which, at this stage of his analysis of the concept of a rational being and agent, is the linchpin of his entire philosophical rather than common-sensical derivation of the categorical imperative.

But Kant does not immediately offer us anything else that looks like an argument for the thesis that rational being and its exemplification in human beings is an end in itself, so we will have to leave this question hanging for now. We still have to confront the other question Kant's statements thus far have left unanswered, namely what exactly is it to treat a human being, whether oneself or someone else, as an end and not merely as a means? As we noted, Kant does not offer us a helpful definition of humanity or rational being here. So there are two ways to proceed: we can see if he offers us a helpful definition elsewhere, and we can see what we can infer from his examples of what it is to treat or fail to treat rational being as an end in itself.

Kant does provide some definitions elsewhere of what he means by 'humanity' specifically. In the Introduction to the 'Doctrine of

Virtue' in the *Metaphysics of Morals* – where, it will be recalled, he is deriving specifically human duties from the general principle of morality, so he can talk of 'humanity' as the human exemplification of rational being in general and no longer needs to talk directly about rational being as such – he says that humanity is that aspect of human nature, in contrast to the 'crudeness' of its 'animality,' 'through which alone' the human being 'is capable of setting ends for himself' (*MM*, 'Doctrine of Virtue,' Introduction, section V.A., 6:387). Several pages later he similarly says that what is characteristic of humanity, in contrast to animality, is 'the capacity to set oneself any end in general' (section VIII.1, 6:392). And in the *Groundwork* itself, he says in more general terms that 'Rational nature distinguishes itself from the rest in that it sets itself an end. This would be the matter for every good will' (4:437). In other words, rational being, whether in general or in its specifically human manifestation, is the ability to set one's own ends rather than have them determined by anything other than one's own choice, whether that be one's own mere impulses or the arbitrary choices of another. Thus to make humanity or rational being whether in oneself or anyone else the object, or as Kant here says, the matter of one's will (again confirming that his 'formal' moral principle is not one that has no relation to ends at all, but only one that does not depend upon arbitrary and subjective ends), means to treat the capacity of every human being as a rational being and of every rational being more generally (if there are any others and if we in any way interact with them) *to make his own choices of ends* as the sole thing of unconditional value, not to be restricted or compromised by any particular end of merely conditional value but rather itself to restrict the pursuit of all particular ends. But this is just to say that it is the *freedom* of each human or rational being to choose his own ends that is the thing of unconditional value that is the basis of the categorical imperative. Thus, although using different language, Kant arrives at the same conclusion as his pre-*Groundwork* moral theory, namely that freedom, at least in the choice of ends, is the end, and universal laws of reasons must be the means to achieve this end.

That what Kant means by the unconditional value of humanity is the inviolability of the freedom of each to choose his own ends is also what is suggested by his illustrations of FEI. Kant uses the same examples of duties to confirm the correctness of his formulation of FEI that he previously used to confirm FUL/FLN, and again we will defer until later in this chapter the more detailed discussion of these examples. But let's take a quick look now at the cases we briefly discussed before, namely the duty not to make false promises to others and the duty of beneficence. Kant previously explained the wrongness of false promises by saying that the universalization of one's intention to make such promises would undermine one's ability to use a false promise for one's own purposes because it would undermine the institution of promising altogether. Here he says that to make a false promise to another human being is to use him merely as a means to one's own ends without allowing him 'at the same time to contain the end in himself'; more fully, one who would transgress the rights of others by making false promises 'is of a mind to use the person of others merely as a means, without considering that they, as rational beings, must always be esteemed as at the same time an end, i.e., as able to contain in themselves the end of the very same action' (4:429–30). That is, to make a false promise is to deprive the promisees of the ability to choose to accept your end and make it their own freely because it forces them to operate with false information about your intentions, and to that extent under duress; conversely, to treat others as ends in themselves is to ensure that they will consent to your action and make it their own end as well only in a situation where they have all the information about your intentions that you do and thus can set their own ends as freely as you can set yours. Thus to treat others as ends in themselves is to ensure that in the face of your action they retain what is essential to their own humanity, namely the right to set their own ends freely or to make the ends of others their own by freely consenting to them.

This example illustrates one important point about FEI, namely that it does not prohibit treating others as ends altogether, but only treating them *merely* as ends. For when you make a sincere and honest promise to someone else, you *are* treating that person as a means to your own end, for example of getting the money that you will obtain from the other through that promise; but insofar as you allow the other to accept your promise freely, without any misinformation or other form of duress, you are allowing her to accept the promise only if she sees doing so as in her own interest, consistent with her own freely chosen ends. So in making an honest instead of a false promise, you are not treating the other *merely* as a means, but are respecting her own freedom of choice and thus her own humanity while still using her as a means to your own end.

Kant's illustration of FEI by the duty of beneficence suggests another important point about his conception of humanity. Here he says that although 'humanity could subsist if no one made any contribution to the happiness of others,'

> this is only a negative and not a positive agreement with **humanity as an end in itself** if everyone does not also, as far as he can, try to further the ends of others. For the ends of the subject who is an end in itself must, if that representation is to have **all** of its effect on me, also be so far as possible **my** ends. (4:430)

What this implies is that treating others as ends in themselves is not exhausted simply by doing nothing to deprive them of the capacity to choose their own ends or to restrict their ability to exercise this capacity freely. Treating others as ends in themselves also requires furthering their particular ends, or helping them realize those ends, as far as one can. Just what that last qualification means needs to spelled out: it will certainly mean helping them to achieve their particular ends only when so doing is consistent with one's other duties, and perhaps also with realizing one's own legitimate ends. But the important point for the moment is that Kant's account of this positive duty means that humanity must be not just the ability to set one's ends freely but also the ability to pursue their realization freely and effectively as far as is possible. If humanity is the ability both to choose ends freely and pursue them effectively, then treating humanity as an end and never merely as a means requires both preserving freedom of choice in oneself and others and promoting the development of the capacities to pursue those ends.

Kant's conception of positive duties toward humanity requires us to be careful in how we interpret his remarks that the unconditional value of humanity as an end in itself is to be 'the supreme limiting condition on the freedom of the actions of every human being' (4:431) and further that this end 'must not be conceived of as an end to be effected, **but as a self-sufficient** end, hence only negatively' (4:437). These remarks might seem to imply that FEI can give rise only to negative duties, duties not to injure or restrict the freedom of others, but this cannot be what Kant means. Rather, what he means is in the first instance that the unconditional value of the capacity of all human beings to set their own ends and pursue them effectively must be a limiting condition on one's own pursuit of one's own more particular ends: only insofar as the latter is consistent with the former is it permissible for one to pursue one's own particular ends. Kant's further suggestion that rational being is not an end 'to be effected' may mean that, unlike other ends, rational being is not something that has to be brought into existence – it is already there in the person of oneself and every other human being. Thus, one does not have a special duty to produce rational beings (and Kant never suggests that any human being has a duty to reproduce). But the claim that rational being is not itself an end 'to be effected' cannot mean that one does not have a positive duty to further or effect the realization of the particular ends freely chosen *by* rational beings or by human beings in the exercise of their humanity, for that is a duty that Kant has explicitly said that we do have.

The positive duty to assist in realizing or effecting the particular ends of rational beings is also assumed in Kant's characterization of the 'realm of ends.' So let us now turn to the next stage of Kant's exposition of the categorical imperative, which will culminate in this characterization of our moral end.

iv. *Autonomy and the realm of ends*

Kant sums up the exposition of the categorical imperative thus far and introduces its next stage in the following words:

> The ground of all practical legislation lies **objectively in the rule** and the form of universality, which (in accordance with the first principle) makes it capable of being a law (a possible law of nature), **subjectively**, however, in the **end**; the subject of all ends however is every rational being as an end in itself (in accordance with the second principle): from this now follows the third practical principle of the will, as the supreme condition of its agreement with universal practical reason, the idea **of the will of every rational being as a universally legislating will**. (4:431)

The first part of this sentence reiterates Kant's claim that in the first instance the categorical imperative requires nothing but the universalizability of any morally acceptable maxim, or more precisely the consistency of acting on a maxim, which itself may be suggested by inclination, with the universalization of that maxim, which is what is demanded by morality. The second part reiterates Kant's claim that a rational will is always moved to its choice of an action, including its choice to accept a law, by the value of an end to which that action is the means, but that the moral will must be moved by an unconditionally valuable end – by using the phrase 'the subject of all ends' Kant signals that this end must be unconditional – and that this unconditional end can be nothing but the absolute value of every rational being as an end in itself. But what does the 'third practical principle,' the 'idea of the will of every rational being as a universally legislating will,' add to the first two claims?

In one sense, it adds no new substantive demand of morality, as indeed neither of the first two claims is supposed to add a substantively new demand to the other: Kant's conception of the relation between the first two main practical principles, that is, FUL/FLN on the one hand and FEI on the other, is that treating *every* person as an end in him- or herself (FEI) requires acting only on maxims that all could accept and, if, they also wish, act upon (FUL/FLN), while conversely acting only upon maxims that all could accept and act upon guarantees that you will be treating every person as an end.[5] The main reason why Kant had to add FEI to FUL/FLN was not to add to our duties but to explain the ground or reason for accepting FUL/FLN. Similarly, Kant's third practical principle does not actually add to our duties, but further explicates what is implied by acting on FUL/FLN; indeed, as it turns out, Kant's 'third practical principle' will explicate more fully both the reason for accepting FUL/FLN and also the outcome of accepting it.

The first point that Kant makes, the point that is explicit in the 'idea of the will of every rational being as a universally legislating will,' is that since, as FEI makes clear, the reason for extending moral treatment to all other persons is their status as *rational* beings, they too must be considered not just as beings who set ends for themselves but also as beings who are capable of doing so rationally, and thus themselves capable of and under the obligation of acting in accordance with universal laws. To treat them as ends in themselves is thus not just to treat them as *subject* to universal laws but as capable of *giving* universal laws, that is, legislating, and of having the right to do so. So to treat everyone as ends in themselves (FEI) must also be to treat them as themselves legislators of the universal laws that are applied to them (FUL/FLN). As Kant puts it, 'The will [of each person] will therefore not merely be subjected to the law, but subjected in such a way that he too can be regarded **as self-legislating** and on that account first subjected to the law (of which he can consider himself the author)' (4:431). And this means that by regarding all others under the light of FEI and for that reason submitting one's own maxims to the test of FUL/FLN, one will not merely be preserving the freedom of all to set their own particular ends but also the freedom of all to author or at least consent to the laws that apply to them. Here is where Kant introduces the originally political term 'autonomy,' saying that we can call this third principle 'the principle of the **autonomy** of the will, in contrast to every other, which I therefore count as a principle of **heteronomy**' (4:433). In using this political term, Kant suggests that he is thinking of the argument of Jean-Jacques Rousseau's *Social Contract*, where Rousseau sums up his argument that people must give up the lawless freedom of entirely individual preference for the 'civil freedom' that they gain by living under laws to which they have freely consented by saying that 'The people, being subject to the laws, ought to be their author.'[6]

Kant also uses the idea of each person being a legislator of the moral laws to which he or she is subject to give a further characterization of the reason that we have as rational beings for accepting the moral law (assuming that we are capable of being rational beings, which, as Kant once again points out, has yet to be proven; see the end of 4:431). Kant argues that a will that is bound to a law merely by an 'interest' can never be bound to a truly universal law, for to be bound to a law by an interest is to be bound to it by self-love, which will lead a person to abide by a law only insofar as he sees it in his self-interest to do so – and one can always imagine circumstances in which it seems to be in one's self-interest to evade a law. Kant is not very explicit about what he means, but he speaks of 'interest as a stimulus or coercion' (4:433), and thus seems to mean that to be bound to observance of a law by interest and self-love is to be bound to it only by the desire for reward or the fear of punishment – and those will never give anyone reason to accept a truly universal law, for there will always be circumstances in which it may seem likely that neither the promised reward nor the promised punishment will be forthcoming, and that self-love or self-interest would therefore be better served by evading the law rather than by complying with it. But if one thinks of oneself as the author or legislator of the law, then one has an entirely different sort of reason for complying with it, namely the thought that by this law 'one is bound to act only in accordance with one's own will, although with a will that is in accordance with its natural end universally legislating' (4:432). Using another one of Kant's metaphors, we might say that one's reason for accepting and abiding by the moral law will be one's pride in its authorship rather than a mere hope for reward or fear of punishment. Kant's thought is that this pride of authorship will give one a reason to accept the law wholeheartedly and without reservation, not merely conditionally as one accepts it if one accepts it merely from self-love.[7] Thus, just as thinking of all persons, oneself and others, as ends in themselves gives one reason to accept FUL/FLN in one's treatment of oneself and others, so thinking of both oneself and others as free legislators of the moral law gives one further reason to think of others as entitled to the protection of FUL/FLN and of oneself as having reason to accept FUL/FLN always as opposed to only when it seems consistent with self-love or self-interest.

That all should be conceived of as a legislators of the laws that bind them seems one thing that can be extracted from the concept of rational agents. In his exposition of the third practical principle Kant implies another consideration that might also be thought to follow from the concept of the subjects of morality as rational agents. For he does not just say that we must consider *each* of our maxims as if it were to be a law legislated by all, but also describes the third principle as 'the **principle** of every human will as **that of a will legislating universally through all of its maxims**' (4:432) and says that 'the concept of every rational being . . . must consider itself as universally legislating through all the maxims of its will' (4:432). What Kant seems to have in mind here is that a rational being does not merely act in accordance with its own representation of a law considered in isolation, but also seeks *consistency* or *systematicity*, and thus acts only in accordance with a representation of *all* of its laws as comprising a coherent and systematic whole. This means that a rational being will not just ask whether a particular maxim on which it proposes to act treats itself and every other rational being as ends in themselves (FEI) and will therefore check whether *that* maxim could be universalized and if desired acted upon by everyone (FUL/FLN); it will also ask whether any particular maxim on which it proposes to act could be part of a coherent system of maxims on which it and all others could act. If there are some maxims that could pass the test of being universalized in a thought-experiment where they are the only maxims that are being considered, then perhaps this will seem to impose a stronger constraint on morally acceptable maxims than FUL/FLN alone; but if a full notion of rationality is already being assumed by FEI, then this requirement will not in fact add to the moral constraints that were already at least implicit in the first two formulations of the categorical imperative. Be that as it may, we can conclude this discussion of Kant's first way of formulating the 'third practical principle' by saying that while it might seem a bit odd to think of the requirement of systematicity as a constituent of autonomy, if we keep in mind the original political sense of that word we will remember that an autonomous city or state is one that freely determines the whole body of its legislation, not one that has merely been given discretion over some issues of primarily local concern. So perhaps having both the freedom and the responsibility to develop a completely coherent body of legislation is part of the meaning of autonomy after all.

I referred a moment ago to Kant's *first* formulation of the 'third practical principle,' because Kant actually describes the third principle in two different ways. As we saw, he has said that the principle that everyone must be treated as the co-legislator of any maxims and indeed of the system of all the maxims on which one proposes to act can be called the 'principle of autonomy' (4:433), or the Formula of Autonomy (FA). But he then says that

> The concept of every rational being that must consider itself as legislating universally through all the maxims of its will in order to judge itself and its actions from this point of view leads to a very fruitful concept attached to it, namely that of **a realm of ends**, (4:433)

and he subsequently refers to the 'formula' that 'All maxims from one's own legislation should harmonize into a possible realm of ends, as a realm of nature' (what we can call the Formula of the Realm of Ends or FRE), rather than FA, as the 'third way' of 'representing the principle of morality' (4:436). So now we must ask, what does Kant mean by a realm of ends and why does he says that FRE follows directly from FA, which in turn, as we have seen, follows, along with FUL/FLN, from FEI?

Kant quickly makes clear what he means by a 'realm of ends.' First he says that it is 'the systematic combination of different rational beings through common laws.' But then he adds that, even though 'one abstracts from the personal differences of rational beings, including all content of their private ends,' in order for laws 'to determine ends in accordance with their universal validity,' a realm of ends is 'a whole of all ends (both of rational beings as ends in themselves and of the particular ends that each may set for himself) in systematic connection' (4:433). What he means is that, on the one hand, each member of a community of moral legislators must abstract from his or her private ends *in legislating the universally valid laws* of the community in order to ensure that those laws truly are universally valid, but, on the other, that what those laws will do is not only ensure that each member of the community is treated as an end in himself but also allow each member to pursue his own ends insofar as so doing is consistent with the general laws of the community and with others pursuing their own ends insofar as they are consistent with those laws, and indeed the laws will require each member to assist the others in so doing insofar as that is in their power and consistent with their own observation of the general laws. Why? Because to treat each person as an end in himself, or more precisely each person's humanity as an end in itself, is to treat each person's ability to set her own ends freely and pursue them effectively as an end in itself and a limiting condition on all other choices. Thus, the first part of the concept of a realm of ends – that is, the requirement to establish a whole of rational beings as ends in themselves – entails the second part – that is, the requirement to promote a systematic and coherent whole of the particular ends that each may set for herself. Determining the laws of the realm of ends requires abstracting from private ends, but actually establishing a realm of ends requires promoting the realization of a systematic whole of private ends. In this way, we might say that FRE follows from FEI as well as from FA, the latter understood as the requirement to act only on maxims that could be part of a systematic body of legislation freely authored by all; but since FA itself follows from FEI, we could also say that both FA and FRE bring out the full implications of FEI, FA emphasizing the character of the laws that would result from FEI and FRE describing more fully the whole state of affairs, particular actions as well as laws, that would result from FEI.

Kant himself sums up the relations among his various formulations of the categorical imperative thus:

> The three ways of representing the principle of morality that have been adduced are at bottom only so many formulae of one

and the same law, one of which unifies the others in itself.
Nevertheless there is a difference among them, which is to be sure
rather subjective than objective-practical, namely, in order to
bring an idea of reason closer to intuition and thereby to feeling
(by means of a certain analogy). All maxims have namely
1) a **form**, which consists in universality, and there the formula of
the moral imperative is expressed thus: that maxims must be so
chosen as if they were to hold as universal laws of nature;
2) a **matter**, namely an end, and there the formula says: that the
rational being, as by its nature an end, hence as an end in itself,
must serve every maxim as a restricting condition on all merely
relative and arbitrary ends;
3) **a complete determination** of all maxims through that formula,
namely: that all maxims from one's own legislation should harmonize into a possible realm of ends, as a realm of nature.

He continues:

There is a progression here through the categories of the **unity** of
the form of the will (its universality), the **multiplicity** of the
matter (the objects, i.e., the ends), and the **allness** or totality of the
system thereof. But one does better if in moral judging one always
proceeds in accordance with the strict method and takes as the
ground the universal formula of the categorical imperative: **act in
accordance with that maxim that can at the same time make itself
into a universal law**. But if one would at the same time gain **entry**
for the moral law, then it is very useful to take one and the same
action through all three formulae and thereby bring it, as far as
possible, closer to intuition. (4:436–7)

Several things are clear from this passage, and several less so. On
the one hand, when Kant says that each principle is a way of representing the moral law, he suggests that when applied each principle should give the same results, that is, each should lead to the
same set of particular duties. At the same time, when he says that
one principle unites the other two, that seems to refer to the third
principle, which provides the 'complete determination' of all
maxims, in other words to the Formula of the Realm of Ends. This
suggests that both FUL/FLN and FEI should lead, through FA, to
FRE, and that although all of the principles should be coextensive,

FRE makes most explicit everything that morality requires. That would be consistent with the interpretation that has been presented here. On the other hand, when Kant suggests that in actual moral judging one should always use FUL/FLN and that the other formulae should be used merely because their imagery helps the moral law gain entry, presumably to ordinary human beings, he seems to contradict the idea that perhaps FRE should be used in actual moral decision-making because it most explicitly states all of the objectives of morality. And when Kant says in particular that FUL/FLN should be treated as the 'ground' in moral decision-making, that seems to belie what has been argued here, namely that FEI expresses the 'ground of the possibility' of the categorical imperative, and thus provides the reason for accepting the constraint expressed in FUL/FLN and is the basis for both FA and FRE.

The complexities of this passage have attracted much attention,[8] but I propose that we reconcile Kant's statements with the interpretation that has been presented here as follows. The idea that humanity and in general every rational being should always be treated as an end and never merely as a means, in other words that rational beings are the ultimate 'object' or 'matter' of moral conduct, expresses the absolute value that lies at the basis of morality, and in that sense must be the ground of every other formulation of the categorical imperative – the statement of value that makes acting in accordance with the other formulations rational. Reflection on what fully respecting the humanity or rational being of *every* person requires leads to the ideas of autonomy and the realm of ends, that is, the idea that every person must be regarded as a co-legislator of the whole system of laws that binds all but within which each must be allowed to pursue her ends consistent with those laws and indeed each must be assisted in so doing insofar as that is possible. Thus FA and FRE describes what should be the outcome of fully accepting FEI – an outcome that will no doubt be 'only an ideal,' as Kant says (4:433), because of the imperfection of the human beings who will try to bring it about, but which nevertheless should be the goal of all of our conduct. But since we cannot actually think of all the laws that apply to a community of agents and of all their individual ends at once, we may do best in any particular situation in which we need to make a moral decision to test the particular maxim on which we propose to act by FUL/FLN. Of course, all of this will work only if

FUL/FLN really does give rise to precisely the same set of actual duties that we could derive from FEI or from its derivatives, FA and FRE.

3. THE BASIS FOR KANT'S ARGUMENT

At this point, before we turn more fully to Kant's examples of duties, we need to step back from the analysis of the categorical imperative that we have just gone through and ask whether Kant has any argument in its behalf, or if the whole thing hangs on the bald assertion that 'the human being and in general every rational being **exists** as an end in itself' (4:428).

We saw in Chapter 2 that in other writings leading up to *Groundwork*, Kant held that *freedom* is the end and that adherence to universal laws is mandated as the only possible means to that end. One way of asking our present question is by asking whether Kant is tacitly employing that argument within the *Groundwork*, but doing so consistently with the methodological constraint that he has imposed upon himself, namely that of establishing a completely pure and *a priori* principle of morality.

i. *Humanity and freedom*

In the discussion of the formula of humanity as an end in itself in the previous section, we have already seen that Kant's concept of humanity is at the very least closely related to his concept of freedom. In the Introduction to the 'Doctrine of Virtue' of the *Metaphysics of Morals*, we saw, he defines humanity as the ability to set one's own ends, which is certainly a central component of any conception of freedom, and in his illustrations of the duties that arise from the imperative always to treat humanity as an end and never merely as a means in the *Groundwork*, as we saw from our preliminary discussion of these examples, he argues that what must be done in order to comply with that demand is to ensure that in any interaction with another agent that agent's right to consent to the aims of the action freely is preserved, without misinformation and duress, and in that sense to make the ends of the action his own, in other words to ensure that the freedom of choice of all affected by an action or its maxim is preserved. Further, as we saw from Kant's discussion of the duty of beneficence, the principle of humanity also requires that we do what we can to make agents' choices of ends efficacious, that is, to help them realize their ends; we must not just allow all agents freedom of choice, but must help them make their freedom of choice effective. Our more detailed discussion of Kant's illustrations of the principle in the next section will make it clear that in the case of duties to oneself the principle of treating the humanity in one's own person as an end and never merely as a means also mandates both the preservation of one's own freedom of choice and making one's own choice of ends efficacious: the duty to refrain from suicide, we will see, is the duty to refrain from destroying a free being capable of setting its own ends, and (an example we have not yet mentioned) the duty to cultivate one's talents is the duty to take steps to make one's free choices of ends, whatever those might turn out to be, efficacious. So in general the duty to make humanity an end and never merely a means seems to be equivalent to the duty to preserve freedom of choice whether in others or oneself and whenever it is in one's power to take sufficient steps to make particular free choices effective.

There is clearly, then, a close relation between the concept of humanity as an end in itself and the concept of freedom of choice and action. However, several of Kant's examples as well as his use of the political term 'autonomy' to describe the ultimate aim of moral conduct might suggest that the kind of freedom he has in mind in the formulations of the categorical imperative in Section II of the *Groundwork* is primarily *the freedom of the choice of one person from interference by the choice of another person*, and that this is not as general a conception of freedom as that which he employed in his other writings up to the time of the *Groundwork*. Thus it might seem as if the argument of *Groundwork* II is not the same as the argument that he sketched out in these other texts that adherence to universal laws is necessary as the only means to free oneself from determination by mere impulse or inclination.

For several reasons, however, this conclusion should be resisted. First, the freedom that is threatened by suicide (from the motive of self-love) or by neglecting the development of one's talents is not the freedom of one's choice from interference by the choice of another person, but rather interference with one's *future* freedom of choice by one's own *present* choice, where that present choice cannot be explained except as giving in to mere inclination. That is, the choice to commit suicide just in order to avoid suffering would be a choice to give in to one's present inclination to avoid pain even at the cost of destroying all possibility for one's future freedom of choice at all, and the choice to lay idle instead of working at cultivating one's talents would be the choice to give in to one's present inclination to indolence at the cost of depriving oneself of the talents and skills one may need in the future in order to make one's future choices of ends (or choices to support others in the pursuit of their ends) effective. In these sorts of cases, then, the duty to treat humanity in oneself as an end is equivalent to the duty to determine one's own ends and provide oneself with means for effectively pursuing them rather than letting them be determined by mere impulse. To be sure, a choice such as that to commit suicide or to let one's talents rust is, if considered by itself, as free a choice as any other, a free choice to *give in to* inclination. The moral problem in these cases is not that one does not make a free choice at all, but rather that one makes a free choice to give in to inclination on one occasion that is incompatible with the continued existence and efficacy of one's ability to make free choices on many future occasions. What Kant's formula requires, in other words, is, as the idea of the 'self-consistency' of the use of freedom that we found in his *Lectures on Ethics* suggests, the preservation and promotion of freedom over one's own intrapersonal life span as well as interpersonally. And that certainly does require mastery of one's inclinations (even if not, as Kant mistakenly suggested at *G* 4:428, the complete elimination of all inclinations).

A second point that can be made here, even though Kant does not explicitly make it, is that to allow oneself to be determined by the will of another and thus to violate one's own autonomy is also a decision to allow oneself to be determined by mere inclination, indeed a decision to allow oneself to be doubly determined by inclination. For, first, one's own decision to allow oneself to be determined by the will of the other in a morally prohibited way can only be explained as a decision to give in to an inclination – say, to get a reward from the other or, more likely, avoid some sort of punishment – rather than to preserve and promote one's own freedom. And second, the other's decision to dominate one at the cost of one's own freedom can only be explained as *his* decision to give in to inclination – say, his inclination for domination or self-aggrandizement – rather than to respect humanity in the person of every other as well as in himself. So the violation of autonomy arises from the domination of both parties by inclination, and conversely the preservation of autonomy depends upon the mastery of inclination in all parties. Thus the goal of attaining autonomy throughout a community, or in Kant's terms the goal of realizing a realm of ends, is in fact dependent upon the goal of achieving freedom from domination by impulse and inclination.

Finally, it should be noted that in *Groundwork* II Kant himself frequently equates autonomy with freedom from domination by natural mechanisms, and thus from domination by inclination, even though he does not explicitly make the argument just suggested. Thus he says that if one's action is determined by an interest of stimulus or coercion, then one's will is not determined by a 'law that has arisen from **one's own** will but is necessitated to act in a certain way in accordance with a law from **something else**' (4:433) – not from *someone* else, but from *something* else, that is, from something alien to one's own rationality, which can be nothing other than mere inclination. And similarly he says that what justifies the 'high claims' of the 'morally good disposition' is that in treating oneself as an end in oneself one is thereby 'legislating in the realm of ends, as free with regard to all laws of nature, obeying only those laws that one gives oneself and in accordance with which one's maxims can belong to a universal legislation (to which one at the same time subjects oneself)' (4:435). But to be determined by laws of nature rather than laws that one gives oneself – at least if we are not thinking of a person merely as a physical object, subject to the law of gravitational attraction just like any other body, a stone or projectile – is in Kant's mind to be determined by impulse.

For these reasons, then, it seems clear that although in the *Groundwork* Kant uses the language of humanity and autonomy rather than talking explicitly of freedom from impulse as he did in his other writings, his view has not changed. His central thought remains that freedom of choice, over one's own lifetime and over the lifetimes of all, is our supreme value, and that the role of moral laws, both the categorical imperative in general and the particular duties that derive from it, is to state the means that are necessary to realize this unconditional end.

ii. *Proving that humanity is the only end in itself*
That being said, however, now we must face the question of whether Kant's entire exposition of the categorical imperative rests on the bald assertion 'that the human being and in general every rational

being **exists** as an end in itself' (4:428), or whether he can somehow prove this claim. Again, as Kant frequently reminds us, he will not attempt to prove that *we* are rational beings to whom this principle applies until Section III of the *Groundwork*, so the question here is rather whether he can prove that *any* rational being must accept this principle, or that it is, in his terms, part of the concept of rational being itself, whether he has shown 'through unfolding the generally accepted concept of morality that an autonomy of the will is unavoidably attached to it or rather is its ground' (4:445). We may again divide our discussion of this issue into three points.

    a. A Naturalistic Justification? In other writings leading up to the *Groundwork*, as we saw, Kant often based his derivation of the moral law on the psychological or 'anthropological' fact that human beings love freedom or have the strongest and most satisfying feeling of life when they have the maximal scope for free and unhindered activity. Kant's insistence in the *Groundwork* that the moral law must be pure and *a priori* and cannot be based on any characteristic empirically discovered to be peculiar to human beings clearly means that he cannot in good faith appeal to such a premise in his official analysis of the moral law. Nevertheless, there are several places in the heart of the argument of *Groundwork* II where Kant does say that it is *nature* that determines that humanity must be an end in itself. In the passage leading to the statement of FEI, Kant says that 'rational beings are called **persons** because *their nature* already distinguishes them as ends in themselves' (4:428). In the transitional passage between FEI and FA, he writes that all prior attempts at moral theory (although not, given the argument of *Groundwork* I, prior moral decision-making) have failed because it was not recognized that the human being 'is subjected **only to his own** and yet **universal legislation**, and that he is only bound to act in accordance with his own but *in accordance with the end of nature* universally legislating will' (4:432). And in the passage in which he describes the relation among the three main formulations of the categorical imperative, he states the second formula thus: 'the rational being, *as by its nature an end*, hence as an end in itself, must serve every maxim as a restricting condition on all merely relative and arbitrary ends' (4:436, all italics added). 'Nature' is notoriously one of the slipperiest terms in the philosophical lexicon,[9] so it is far from clear what these allusions to nature mean. But Kant could be saying that it is some sort of fact or law of nature that rationality is unconditionally valuable, even though this is a fact that we are supposed to know *a priori* rather than empirically (that is not by itself self-contradictory, for the whole *Critique of Pure Reason* is after all dedicated to showing that there are certain laws of nature that we can nevertheless know *a priori*). And just one year before the *Groundwork*, in the essay 'Idea for a Universal History from a Cosmopolitan Point of View,' Kant said that 'Nature has willed that the human being should produce entirely out of himself everything that goes beyond the mechanical arrangement of his animal existence and should participate in no other happiness or perfection than what he has himself created, free from instinct, through his own reason' (8:19); this seems to say that nature has determined that we should be free and are entitled to happiness only insofar as we have produced it through the use of our own reason free from instinct or impulse, in other words through our own morality. As we saw in our discussion of Section I of the *Groundwork*, there too Kant appealed to the thought that nature has given us the faculty of reason for a certain purpose. In such remarks, Kant does seem to suppose that it can be a natural fact that we ought to preserve and promote our freedom through adherence to the moral law.

Such an argument may be incredible to the contemporary philosopher who is persuaded that an 'ought' can never be derived from an 'is,' and indeed thinks that this principle originates with Kant himself. It is quite difficult to see how this prohibition could actually be proven, as opposed to being merely a matter of philosophical faith. But it is equally difficult to see how one would go about proving that nature *has* determined morality or anything else as the supreme end for all human beings, let alone all rational beings. Of course, we are not empirically acquainted with any rational beings other than human beings, so we cannot imagine how nature could prove anything about the general class of rational beings rather than the specific class of human beings. But even confining ourselves to human beings, we are certainly acquainted with plenty of them who do not seem to have made morality their supreme end, so it is hard to see in what sense appeal to nature could prove that this is the supreme end for all human beings. So let us leave these allusions to nature aside, at least for the moment, and see if Kant has any other way of proving that freedom or humanity is the absolute and unconditional value for all human beings or even all rational beings.

b. A Metaphysical Justification? Some interpreters have suggested that Kant's thesis that humanity is an end in itself is entailed by the relation between the conditioned and unconditioned, in this case between conditional values and unconditional value, which is a central theme in Kant's metaphysics. This claim, I suggest, is implausible, because it is actually the central theme of Kant's *critique* of metaphysics that, natural as it may be for us to do so, we are not in fact licensed to make an inference from the existence of anything conditioned to the existence of something unconditioned.

This argument has been forcefully expounded by Christine Korsgaard. According to her, Kant holds that if there are only things of conditional value (their value being conferred upon them by the inclinations that they satisfy), then, while one such thing might be valuable as a means to another, there will be an infinite regress, with the value of anything in the regress being dependent upon something else that is of itself merely conditional value. But this means that any claim of value could be rejected by rejecting the thing of merely conditional value from which its value derives, whether by a short chain or a long one. So there must be something of unconditional value, which puts a stop to this regress. But since particular objects of choice, merely as objects of inclination, cannot put a stop to the regress, the only thing that can is the power of rational choice itself: 'what makes the object of your rational choice good is that it is the object of a rational choice. That is, since we still *do* make choices and have the attitude that what we choose is good in spite of our incapacity to find the unconditioned good of the object's goodness in this (empirical) regress upon the conditions, it must be that we are supposing that rational choice itself *makes* its object good.' So the power to make rational choices must itself be unconditionally good and confer conditional value on its particular objects of choice. Further, Korsgaard argues, 'If you view yourself as having a value-conferring status in virtue of your power of rational choice, you must view anyone who has the power of choice as having, in virtue of that power, a value-conferring status,' and you must therefore view humanity, whether in your own person or that of any other, as having unconditional value.[10]

Korsgaard's conclusion that particular ends which would otherwise be mere objects of inclination with no claim on anyone but those whose inclinations they would satisfy must derive their claim to be ends for others from the unconditional value of the humanity of the those who make them their ends is right; the reconstruction of the argument for the moral significance of the realm of ends as a systematic whole of both persons as ends in themselves and of the particular ends that they set for themselves that was offered earlier in this chapter depends upon this premise. But there are problems with Korsgaard's reconstruction of the argument leading to this conclusion. First, there is the risk of circularity, that is, of assuming that *rational* choice has moral value because being rational *means* being moral, so a conception of moral value is actually presupposed by the argument. The interpretation of Kant's argument from the value of freedom to the moral law that has been offered in this book, by contrast, does not presuppose that only the moral or rational use of choice has value; it assumes that free choice as such has value, but that only the regulation of that choice by the moral law *preserves* and *maximizes* that value over the life of one agent and over the lives of all agents. Second, Korsgaard's interpretation misrepresents the structure of Kant's argument. Kant does worry about the possibility of an infinite regress of merely conditional values, thus that if value did always arise only from an interest of stimulus or coercion, 'then the imperative must always have come out as conditioned and not as fit for a moral command at all' (4:433). And he does suppose that it is only if the 'legislation itself that determines all value' has 'a dignity, i.e., unconditioned, incomparable worth' that particular objects can have value with a real claim on all rational beings, for 'nothing has a value' with such a claim 'except that which the law determines for it' (4:436). But Kant cannot be inferring simply that because there would be an infinite regress of values unless there were something of unconditional value, therefore there must be something of unconditional value. For him to make such an inference would be for him to assume the 'principle that when the conditioned is given, then so is the whole series of conditions subordinated one to the other, which is itself unconditioned, also given' (*PureR*, A 307–8/B 364), which is, however, the fundamental sort of metaphysical error or 'transcendental illusion.' Rather, Kant argues in his critique of metaphysics, pure reason may form the 'transcendental idea' of the unconditioned (of the soul as the unconditioned subject, of the world-whole as the unconditioned series, or of God as the unconditioned ground of all events and even all possibilities; *PureR*, A 334/B 391), but it is up to the ordinary cognitive faculties of sensibility and understanding to determine to what extent those ideas can be exemplified in our actual experience (the answer to which is: never completely). Likewise in the moral case, while we may need something of unconditional value to stop an infinite regress of merely conditional values, that by itself does not imply that there actually *is* anything with unconditional value. We need an independent argument that there is something with unconditional value in order to stop the regress. So *if* humanity is an end in itself with unconditional value, that fact will stop the infinite regress of merely conditional values, but *that* it is still needs to be proven.

So the metaphysical argument expounded by Korsgaard is inconsistent with Kant's own critique of metaphysics as well as possibly being circular in its own right. Nevertheless, Kant does make one point that might be considered a metaphysical argument in behalf of his assumption of the unconditional value of humanity as an end in itself. At the outset of *Groundwork* I, it will be remembered, he argued that the good will is the only thing of unconditional value because it is the only thing the value of which does not depend upon circumstances. Returning to the concept of the good will at the conclusion of his exposition of the formulations of the categorical imperative in *Groundwork* II, he says:

> Now we can end where we set out in the beginning, namely with the concept of an unconditionally good will. That **will** is **absolutely good** which cannot be evil, hence whose maxim, when it is made into a universal law, cannot contradict itself. This principle is thus also its supreme law: always act in accordance with that maxim, the universality of which as a law you can at the same time will; this is the only condition under which a will can never be in conflict with itself.

And since he next argues that

> The principle: act in relation to every rational being (to oneself and others) so that in your maxim it also counts as an end in itself, is at bottom the same with the principle: act in accordance with a maxim that at the same time contains its own universal validity for every rational being (4:437),

he is committed to the position that acting on the formula of humanity as an end in itself is in fact the only way to avoid contradiction and self-destruction of the will (although not the only way to describe how to do this). That is, the only way to guarantee that the good will remains self-consistent and thereby remains good, and in that sense is necessarily good, is to act in accordance with FEI (and hence FUL/FLN, FA, and FRE).

This connects Kant's informal or common-sense idea of the good will with his original insight that the only way for the will or the use of freedom to be self-consistent is for it to adhere to the moral law. Of course, it might be argued that there would be no unconditional value in the will or the use of freedom remaining self-consistent and thus preserving itself *unless it was already assumed that the will or the use of freedom is intrinsically valuable.* In other words, although the present consideration avoids the outright inconsistency with Kant's critique of metaphysics from which Korsgaard's reconstruction of his argument for the unconditional value of humanity suffers, it may still be question-begging.

We will see in the next chapter that in Section III of the *Groundwork* Kant does introduce what is clearly a metaphysical argument to prove both that the categorical imperative applies to us human beings and that we are capable of acting in accordance with it. That is a very different argument from the one that Korsgaard ascribes to Kant in Section II or that Kant himself hints at in the conclusion of the section: it does not just assume that an infinite regress of values must be stopped by an unconditional value, but appeals to a metaphysical account of our identity to prove that our real self will act in accordance with the categorical imperative. Of course, that argument will have its own problems.

c. A Normative Justification? For the moment, it seems as if we may have to give up on the hope for either a metaphysical or an empirical and naturalistic justification of Kant's fundamental claim that humanity has absolute value. What remains then is the possibility that the unconditional value of humanity as an end in itself is somehow a self-evident *normative* proposition, that is, that its value is simply self-evident. Kant may be relying on the self-evidence of the value of freedom as the self-determination of the will in his repeated claims that nothing else has genuine 'dignity' and 'sublimity.' He uses this terminology at least six times in *Groundwork* II:

> Everything empirical is, as an addition to the principle of morality, not only entirely unfit for that, but highly disadvantageous to

the purity of morals themselves, where the genuine value of an absolutely good will, sublime above all price, consists in the principle of action being free from all influences of contingent grounds that can be given only in experience. (4:426)

Reason relates every maxim of the will as universally legislative to every other will and also to every action regarding oneself . . not for the sake of some other practical motive or future advantage, but from the idea of the **dignity** of a rational being that obeys no law except that which it at the same time gives itself. (4:434)

Now morality is the condition under which alone a rational being can be an end in itself, for only through it is it possible to be a legislating member in the realm of ends. Thus morality and humanity insofar as it is capable of that is what alone has dignity. (4:435)

And now what is it that justifies the morally good disposition or virtue in making such high claims? It is nothing less than the **share** that it creates for the rational being in the **universal legislation** . . . to which it is already determined by its own nature as an end in itself . . free with regard to all laws of nature, obeying only those that it gives itself . . . The legislation itself, which determines all value, must for that reason have a dignity, i.e., an unconditioned, incomparable value . . . (4:435–6)

The dignity of humanity as rational nature, without any other end or advantage that is to be obtained through it, hence respect for a mere idea, should nevertheless serve as the unremitting precept of the will, and . . precisely in this independence of maxims from all such incentives does their sublimity consist and the worthiness of every rational being to be a legislating member in the realm of ends . . (4:439)

For there is no sublimity in a person to the extent that he is **subjected** to the moral law, but there certainly is insofar as with regard to that law he is at the same time **legislating** and only for that reason subordinated to it. (4:440)

The hortatory character of Kant's language in all of these passages is unmistakable. We are simply supposed to be stirred by the idea of freely determining our own laws and setting our own ends instead of being controlled by laws of nature and pushed around by mere inclinations, and to realize that there is nothing more important than that, even though we must also realize that we must govern our conduct by universalizable and systematic maxims if we are to avoid domination by natural forces such as impulse and inclination. There is no further argument that can be given for this normative claim, although it is the basis for all our duties. Perhaps at this point all we can say is that many people have been stirred by Kant's characterization of the moral ideal, certainly more so than by any other formulation of the fundamental principle of morality in modern times, and indeed many people have been so stirred by the idea of the absolute value of freedom that they have been willing to sacrifice everything so that if not they then their children or compatriots can enjoy it.

We will see in the next chapter that in Section III Kant actually attempts to *sidestep* the question of why we *ought* to accept the idea that humanity has absolute value by arguing that we *are* rational beings who really have no choice but to accept this idea. This will be a metaphysical argument, but very different from the one Korsgaard ascribes to Kant. If it fails, then we may have no choice but either to accept the original psychological basis for morality that Kant tries to leave behind in the *Groundwork* or to accept that the value of humanity is simply self-evident. We can therefore defer further discussion of this issue, and now take up the task of examining in detail Kant's examples of the categorical imperative and the objections they have raised.

4. APPLYING THE CATEGORICAL IMPERATIVE

i. The four examples of duty

Kant provides four examples of the application of the categorical imperative, and discusses these examples twice, once after the statement of FUL/FLN and once after the statement of FEI. He does not go over the examples again after the statements of FA and FRE, consistently with his own statement that it is FUL/FLN that should typically be the method of applying the categorical imperative and with our interpretation of FRE as describing the outcome of following the categorical imperative rather than the method of applying it; but the fact that he does restate the examples after the statement of FEI could raise problems for his claim that FUL/FLN is always the preferred method of application, and we will see that some of Kant's examples tacitly appeal to FA as well as FUL/FLN and/or FEI. It will be recalled from the conclusion of the Preface to the *Groundwork* that the discussion of these examples is intended to be a 'synthetical' moment in the argument for the supreme principle of morality, in which the 'examination of it and its sources' will turn back to the 'common cognition in which its use is found' (4:392). So the examples of duties that Kant discusses are supposed to be non-controversial ones that any successful moral theory would have to be able to derive, and the success of Kant's version of the moral principle in deriving these duties is supposed to be at least part of its confirmation. Kant's examples are also chosen to be comprehensive. In first introducing the examples after the statement of FUL/FLN, he says that 'We will now enumerate some duties, in accordance with their customary division into duties toward ourselves and duties toward other people, and into perfect and imperfect duties' (4:421). The combination of these two distinctions would give rise to four classes of duties: perfect duties toward oneself, perfect duties toward others, imperfect duties toward oneself, and imperfect duties toward others. The contrast between duties toward oneself and duties toward others is self-evident. Kant explains the distinction between perfect and imperfect duties as the distinction between 'those that permit no exceptions for the sake of inclination' (4:421n.) and those that, by implied contrast, do; we will see in section 5 of this chapter that this is a misleading description of the distinction. But let us not worry about that for the moment; the point for now is just that Kant takes the two distinctions, between duties to self and duties toward others and between perfect and imperfect duties, however exactly the latter distinction is to be explained, to be commonly accepted, and likewise the fourfold classification that arises from combining them. So if he can show that his version of the moral principle yields a representative or even better paradigmatic example of each of these four classes of duty, then he will have gone some way toward the 'synthetical' confirmation of that principle. He says that he will reserve the complete division of duties for 'a future *Metaphysics of Morals*,' presumably meaning by this that he will save both a more complete explanation of the principle of division, especially the distinction between perfect and imperfect duties, as well as a more complete enumeration and derivation of duties from the general principle of morality for that later work, and that because he will address those issues of detail later 'it is all the same to him' whether the present division is 'conceded' (4:421n.). But obviously the present examples are carefully chosen as both important and illustrative duties whose successful derivation from Kant's version of the categorical imperative will lend it important support.

a. Suicide. Kant's first example is a perfect duty toward oneself, namely the prohibition of suicide, more precisely the prohibition of suicide from the principle or motive of self-love, specifically in order to avoid continued suffering. Kant considers the case of someone who has suffered such a 'series of evils' that he has now become hopeless and weary of life, but retains enough 'possession of reason' to ask himself whether it would not be contrary to his duty toward himself to take his own life. In the first discussion of this example, following the statement of FUL/FLN, Kant describes such a person as 'testing whether his maxim could well be a universal law of nature. His maxim, however, is: From self-love I make it my principle to shorten my life if its longer duration threatens more evil than it promises agreeableness.' Thus Kant asks whether 'this principle of self-love could become a universal law of nature.' He then says it could not, because 'a nature whose law it was to destroy life itself through the same feeling whose vocation it is to impel the furtherance of life would contradict itself' (4:421–2). This is a peculiar and not very convincing argument: Kant does not ask what we expect him to ask, namely whether there would be a contradiction between one person's acceptance of this maxim and everyone's accepting it, that is, he does not ask what would be the consequence of the universalization of the maxim, and instead bases his argument on the dubious teleological principle that any natural phenomenon, for example the feeling of self-love, can have one and only one function in all possible circumstances. As we have noted before, on Kant's own interpretation of teleology in the subsequent *Critique of the Power of Judgment*, such a principle could at most be a regulative principle for the conduct of inquiry in natural science, and does not seem like an indubitable premise for moral argumentation at all. So Kant's use of the duty against suicide to confirm FUL/FLN does not seem very successful.

Is Kant's use of the prohibition of suicide to illustrate FEI more convincing? Here he says that a person who 'destroys himself in order to escape a burdensome condition uses his own person merely as **a means** for the preservation of a bearable condition to the end of his life,' but that the 'human being is not a thing, hence not something that can be used **merely** as a means,' and must instead 'always be considered as an end in itself in all of its actions' (4:429). The problem with this argument is that the application of the distinction between means and end seems obscure and problematic. We can certainly see what it would mean to say, for example, that someone who grows her hair long merely in order to cut it off and sell it is using her bodily capacity to grow hair merely as a means to some other end. But it is not clear that someone who wants to end her life in order to escape overwhelming pain is treating her existence merely as a means to pleasure; rather, she thinks that her pain makes it impossible to bear continued life, let alone do anything pleasurable *or* otherwise valuable. Conversely, we might argue that someone who insists on preserving her life regardless of her overwhelming pain and incapacity to do anything useful or valuable is treating her continued life merely as a means to the preservation of her rational being in a situation in which the latter can have no value (though this position would threaten Kant's own conviction that rational being *always* has value.) At the very least, Kant's claim here that to commit suicide in these circumstances is to use oneself as a mere means seems insufficiently developed to be convincing.

Does this mean that Kant has no plausible derivation of a prohibition of suicide from the maxim of self-love from his moral principle? This would be too hasty, and in other texts Kant does suggest a more compelling argument than either of the ones thus far considered. In the 'Collins' lectures on ethics, Kant explains what is wrong with suicide in a more illuminating way. First, he notes that 'if the body belonged to life in a contingent way, not as a condition of life but as a state of it, so that we could take it off if we wanted,' or 'slip out of one body and enter another,' then there would be nothing wrong with bodily self-destruction; in other words, he reminds us that the derivation of any particular duty from the general principle of morality, even one so fundamental as the prohibition of suicide, depends upon particular, empirically known features of the human condition. Second, he then explains the problem with suicide: in the actual circumstances of human life, where continued bodily life is necessary to the continued existence of everything human,

117

as soon as someone destroys his body, and thereby takes his life, he has used his free choice in order to destroy the power of free choice itself; but then free choice contradicts itself. If freedom is the condition of life, it cannot be used to abolish life, for then it destroys and abolishes itself; then the human being uses life in order to abolish life itself.[11]

Here Kant says neither that suicide contradicts the character of a law of nature, nor that it is a case of using oneself as a means rather than an end, but that one's use of freedom for this purpose contradicts itself. And by this Kant cannot mean that the act of suicide considered by itself is internally contradictory, both free and unfree, for it is not: it could be a perfectly free choice. What he must mean is that the free act of suicide 'destroys and abolishes' one's *further* life, and therefore, in the circumstances of human existence, where everything depends on life, one's *further* freedom. There is no logical contradiction in doing this, to be sure. There is simply a destruction of the possibility of continued freedom. But if 'humanity' is equivalent to the free power of choice to set one's own ends, as was previously argued, then suicide ordinarily does destroy humanity and thereby fails to respect it, although we do not have to be able to make sense of the idea of suicide as treating oneself as a mere 'means' in order to see this.

'Ordinarily,' note, because there may be cases in which suicide is the best or even the only way to *preserve* or at least *respect* freedom. Kant considers such a case, that of the Roman general and politician Cato (Marcus Porcius Cato Uticensis, 95–46 BCE), who committed suicide in order to prevent himself from being subjected to the imperial ambitions of Julius Caesar and in the hopes of encouraging the other Romans to 'sacrifice their final powers to the defense' of their freedom.[12] We might analyze this as a case in which, first, unfortunate circumstances dictated that Cato, considered by himself, had only one free choice left in his own power, the free choice to commit suicide, for otherwise all his future choices would be dictated by Caesar, and, second, in which Cato's *own* surrender of his future freedom was the only way in which the future freedom of many *other* Romans might actually have been respected and preserved. In other words, when suicide is performed in order to preserve freedom, not out of mere self-love, it might be consistent with duty, or even itself a duty.

Kant does not conclusively endorse Cato's decision, but he says that in such a case suicide at least has a 'plausible side.' Another sort of case in which it might seem at least plausible that suicide is consistent with morality is a case in which a person is facing complete paralysis, say from ALM or 'Lou Gehrig's disease,' and has reached a point where the last free act possible for him before he loses all ability to act or even to make a request of others would be a free act of suicide. Here one might think that the only way to *respect* freedom would be to refuse to live in a state of utter unfreedom and thus to take this step, because it is not mere life itself that is to be treasured and preserved at all costs, but rather the ability 'to live like a human being as long as one lives,'[13] that is, the ability to live *freely*. Of course, if one thinks that the freedom or humanity that has absolute value is strictly an inner condition, freedom of *choice*, the value of which does not rest on the possibility of its outward expression, that is, freedom of *action*, then one might not find this analysis of the case of paralysis convincing; but if one thinks that freedom of action goes hand in hand with freedom of choice as part of 'humanity,' one may.

My suggestion is thus that Kant's prohibition of suicide on the basis of the teleological character of a law of nature or on the requirement that one not treat oneself as a mere means may not be very convincing, but that Kant may have a good argument for the prohibition of suicide from his underlying assumption of the value of freedom itself, although that way of explaining the duty also allows that there may be cases in which suicide is morally permissible or even mandatory. And whether or not one accepts the analysis that has been offered here of the latter cases, they reveal an important point, namely that even in the case of so-called perfect duties, it is not a certain type of action in all possible circumstances that can be prohibited, but only a certain type of action performed for a certain type of reason, or with a certain maxim: suicide out of self-love and the mere desire to avoid further suffering may be prohibited, but suicide in order to prevent the further destruction of freedom in oneself or, failing that, in others may be permitted or even mandatory. It is sometimes offered as an objection to Kant's moral theory that even in the case of perfect duties his categorical imperative does not give rise to completely general prohibitions of action-types, but this seems to be a strength rather than a weakness of his theory's focus not just on actions but on the maxims under which they are performed. For common sense and common law certainly recognize exemptions from even the gravest of prohibitions in the case of certain circumstances and intentions. Thus, homicide is almost always prohibited, but not when it is performed for the sake of national or personal self-defense (although in order to prevent the abuse of this exemption, we restrict the former with strict rules of engagement and place a high burden of proof on claims to the latter). Similarly, theft is almost always prohibited, but breaking into a pharmacy to get life-saving medications in a state of utter emergency might be permitted; and while the law will almost always support the enforcement of promises and contracts, it will not do so when those have been entered into under duress or to bring about an immoral end: if you promise to pay a kidnapper in order to be set free, the law will not hold you to that promise, and if you enter into a contract to enslave yourself or another, neither will the law enforce that (although in the latter case it took quite a while before that became true). So in common morality and law, homicide and false promises are not in fact prohibited in all circumstances, but only when they are performed from certain motives and with certain intentions, while with other motives and intentions they are allowed. Kant's use of the categorical imperative to prohibit actions performed on certain maxims but to allow the performance of outwardly similar actions performed under different maxims is a philosophical expression of this piece of common sense.

This is a good point to keep in mind as we now turn to Kant's example of the prohibition of false promises.

b. False Promises. We have touched upon this example before, but it is worth discussing it again. Unlike his treatments of suicide, Kant's treatments of the duty not to make false promises clearly illustrate how both the test of universalizability and the requirement not to treat persons merely as means are supposed to work.

In his discussion of this example of a perfect duty toward others after his statement of FUL/FLN, Kant poses the question of someone who sees no way out of a financial difficulty except by making a promise to repay borrowed money that he has no intention of keeping. The maxim on which he proposes to act is 'If I believe myself to be in need of money then I will borrow money and promise to repay it back even though I know this will never happen' (4:322). Kant refers to this as a 'principle of self-love' or 'one's own expedience,' terms that express the agent's most fundamental motivation here; so a full statement of the agent's maxim would be something like 'When in financial difficulty (circumstances), then, in order to satisfy my self-love by getting myself out of such a situation (motive), I will borrow money with no intention of repaying it (proposed action).' In order to answer the question of whether acting on such a maxim would be right, however, the agent must 'transform the imputation of self-love into a universal law,' that is, imagine that everyone has adopted their own maxim out of their own self-love, and thus ask 'How would it stand if my maxim were to become a universal law?' According to Kant, the agent would then see immediately that his maxim could not be a universal law of nature but rather would, once universalized, contradict itself, because if everyone were to make false promises (in these circumstances) that would make 'the promise and the end that one would have in it impossible.' As noted earlier, there is no assumption here that one person's adoption of the maxim would actually *cause* others to adopt it; the assumption is rather that if it were to be permissible for one person to act on a maxim then it must be permissible for everyone else to act on it, so the question is whether one could consistently will both one's own maxim and its universalization, that is, everyone else acting upon it, regardless of what might actually cause that to happen. And then one is supposed to see that willing both this maxim and its universalization is impossible, because the universalization of the maxim would destroy a condition of the possibility of acting upon the maxim oneself, namely the existence of the practice of promising. There would not necessarily be a contradiction in acting upon the proposed maxim in the real world, where people often do get away with all sorts of things, but there would be a contradiction in attempting to act upon the maxim in the world that morality requires one to imagine, namely a world in which only universalizable maxims are permissible. Another way of putting this point would be to note that the requirement that one not undermine the condition of the possibility of acting upon one's proposed maxim is actually an implication of the general principle of rationality that also underlies hypothetical imperatives, the principle, namely, that whoever wills the end must also will the means to that end, but that the requirement to consider whether that means would continue to be available if one's maxim were universalized is a specifically moral requirement, or a requirement of pure practical reason rather than practical reason in general.

In his return to this example after his statement of FEI, Kant says that someone who has it in mind to make a deceitful promise to another will immediately see that he 'would be using another person **merely as a means** without the other at the same time containing in himself the end' of the first person's action; 'he whom I would use for my own purposes by means of such a promise cannot possibly consent to my way of treating him and himself contain the end of this action.' Kant says that the same 'conflict with the principle of other human beings' will be even clearer in the cases of 'assaults upon the freedom and property of others,' where it is clear that anyone who would trample the rights of others fails to take account of the fact that 'as rational beings they must always be esteemed as ends, i.e., as ones who must also be able to contain in themselves the end of the very same action' (4:429–30). This gives us a clear account of what it is to treat humanity merely as a means and not at the same time as an end: as humanity is the capacity to set one's own ends freely, of which consenting to the end of an action proposed by another or making that end one's own is one instance, to be forced into performing or suffering an action which may advance the end of another but not any end that one could set or adopt for oneself is to have one's humanity, one's capacity to set ends, treated as a mere means and not as an end in itself. In the simplest terms, for one's humanity always to be treated as an end means that one must be able to consent freely, thus without duress or deceit, to any intended actions and ends – and their underlying maxims – of any others that might in any way affect oneself.

Although it is clear how FUL/FLN and FEI are supposed to be applied in this case, there are several points here that need discussion. First, let us clear away a possible objection to Kant's use of FUL/FLN in a case like that of false promising. Hegel famously argued that at least this version of the categorical imperative is an 'empty formalism,' and that Kant's example works only because it tacitly *presupposes* the moral necessity of a practice such as promising; otherwise there would be no contradiction in a maxim the universalization of which would undermine that practice.[14] A similar recent objection is that there is a 'gap' in FUL/FLN because the test of whether a maxim has 'bare conformity to law as such' does not work, and only testing whether maxims are consistent with specific, presupposed moral laws would be informative – in which case, however, Kant's whole procedure would be circular, presupposing what it is supposed to prove.[15] Such objections fail to see, however, that the contradiction that Kant is worried about is one between a proposed maxim and the universalization of that maxim, and that it is the proposed maxim that presupposes the practice or institution that its own universalization would undermine. That is, *Kant* does not simply presuppose that a moral world must contain the practice of promising or the institutions of property; it is the *agent's* proposed maxim of getting out of a financial scrape by a false promise that presupposes the practice of promising that would be undermined by the universalization of that maxim. Kant is thus not offering a circular argument that a moral world must include the practice of promising; he is showing that *false* promises are impermissible because in a moral world all maxims must be universalizable, but the maxim of making false promises for self-love is not universalizable, because the universalization of this maxim would make it impossible for anyone to act upon it.

This brings up a question that we already touched upon in the discussion of suicide, namely, whether a maxim of making false promises for a reason other than that of self-love might be morally permissible or even morally mandatory in certain circumstances, for example a maxim of making false promises not out of self-love but only in order to save innocent lives out of respect for the value of such lives. Here, common sense would seem to dictate the same approach as before, namely that to make false promises with *this* motive could be right, as in the case of making a false promiser to a kidnapper to pay a ransom in order to save an innocent child. The question would then be whether this sort of maxim could be universalized without undermining the possibility of successfully acting upon it. Would the universalization of the maxim that one can make false promises in order to save innocent lives undermine the institution of promising and thereby undermine the means to the end of one's maxim, or would it be compatible with acting upon that maxim? It is not clear what the answer to this question should be. Perhaps we could argue that occasions in which innocent lives can be saved only by false promises are so rare that the universalization of the maxim to make false promises in but only in such situations would not undermine the practice of promising and thereby render that maxim inconsistent. What would be more likely to render such a maxim unworkable, although not immoral, is that the criminals to whom such false promises would be made know perfectly well what the rare circumstances are in which permissible false promises would be made and will not accept mere promises in such situations – that is why kidnappers won't settle for a mere promise of payment but demand that the ransom actually be dropped off in some safe spot before they release their victims. Be that as it may, it begins to look as if the answer to the question of whether such maxims are permissible must turn on questions that can be answered only empirically rather than *a priori*. It might be easier to approach this question on the basis of FEI rather than FUL/FLN, thus to ask whether any rational person would freely *consent* to a maxim such as that of making false promises when that is the only way to save innocent lives rather than asking whether everyone could actually act upon such a maxim. Here it seems likely that all reasonable persons would freely consent to such a maxim, thus that adopting it is consistent with treating all rational beings as ends and never merely as means.

Which brings us to our second question about Kant's second example, namely whether the requirement of free *consent* to the maxims of others is equivalent to the requirement that morally permissible maxims be *universalizable*, that is, ones that everyone could actually act upon in a logically consistent world. Some commentators interpret the requirement of the *universalizability* of maxims as a requirement of the *universal acceptability* of anyone's maxims, and thus assume that the requirements of universalizability and consent are the same.[16] But it seems easy to think of maxims that seem morally permissible because other people could accept them but which not everyone could actually act upon, for example my maxims always to buy but never to sell antique toy trains or always to play tennis at 10 a.m. on Sunday mornings, when most of the other players who would use the courts will be in church or reading the Sunday paper.[17] My maxim of always playing tennis on Sunday morning when the courts are mostly empty or of being a collector but not a seller of antique model trains seems morally unexceptionable, that is, something that all other reasonable people could accept or to which no reasonable person could object; but if everyone were to act on my maxim of playing tennis on Sunday morning, then my aim of getting to the courts at a time when they are mostly empty would be defeated, and if everyone wanted to buy antique trains but no one wanted to sell them, then my own apparently permissible plan to buy but never to sell would be defeated.

One way of getting around the problem that such maxims seem morally acceptable but do not seem to be universalizable is to say that they need to be more carefully and sincerely formulated. Thus, we might say that in the tennis case, my maxim is really something like 'In order to minimize my waiting time and maximize my playing time, I will always go to the courts when the fewest other people do'; if other players continue to go to church or read the paper and the courts remain free Sunday mornings, then I will continue to go then, but if church attendance or newspaper readership falls off and people start crowding the courts on Sunday mornings, then I will start playing, say, Thursdays at 5:30 p.m., when the others are all going to happy hour. My more general maxim should be not only universally acceptable but also universalizable, as long as there is some time that is the least popular. Or maybe we should say that these maxims are actually conditionals (they are, after all, really hypothetical maxims for the sake of gratifying inclinations): that is, they really have the form of 'If there is a time when the courts are least crowded, then I will play then, but if there is no such time I won't play,' or 'If there are antique toy trains on the market I will buy but never sell, but if there are no sellers then I won't buy.' Then the universalization of my practice might mean I cannot in fact act in my preferred way, but that possibility is already foreseen in my maxim and does not contradict it.

It is not clear whether such a strategy will prove that the universalizability and the universal acceptability of maxims are equivalent. We will return to the question of how maxims should really be formulated shortly, but in order not to delay completing our review of Kant's examples we should defer further discussion for now. Perhaps for the moment we can just say that if FEI is supposed to be the ground or basis for FUL/FLN, then the requirement of the universalizability of my maxims should *follow from* the requirement that *universal free consent* to my maxims must be possible, and that, since of course we cannot know what all present and future human beings, let alone all rational beings, would *actually* consent to, the best way to test for the possibility of universal consent would be to see whether it would be possible for everyone to *act* upon my maxim, that is, whether it is universalizable. We ought to be able to decide this by reasoning from general facts about human or rational nature – such as the fact that normally intelligent human beings as well as other rational beings will not continue to accept promises if false promises are freely made – without having any information about the actual preferences or ends of particular persons. Any maxim that passed the test of universalizability of maxims would certainly be one that it would be possible for everyone actually to consent to, even if their consent to others' adoption of that maxim would not entail that they themselves will actually act upon it. And perhaps this is something that Kant had in mind when he claimed that in the application of the categorical imperative we 'do best' to proceed in accordance with the 'strict method' of FUL/FLN: unlike FEI and its requirement of consent, FUL/FLN, perhaps supplemented by FA, which requires that we test not only the universalizability of our individual maxims but the coherence of our whole set of maxims, can be applied without excessive empirical knowledge of what other people would actually agree to.

c. Cultivating our Talents. Let us now turn to Kant's third case, the duty to cultivate our talents as an example of imperfect duty toward self. In his first treatment of the example, he says that there is no contradiction in the concept of a world in which people prefer to lie around idly gratifying whatever inclinations they can without too much work rather than troubling themselves with the work that would be necessary for the 'expansion and improvement' of their 'fortunate natural predispositions,' but nevertheless it is impossible for a rational being to *will* that a maxim of neglecting the cultivation of one's talents in favor of merely gratifying inclinations 'become a universal law of nature,' 'because as a rational being he necessarily wills that all the capacities in him be developed, because they are serviceable and have been given to him for all sorts of possible ends' (4:423). Kant does not fully spell out the argument he needs here, but he must have in mind that a rational being, again in accordance with the entirely general principle of rationality that whoever wills the end must will adequate means to it, must will the cultivation of human talents if those are the only available means to fulfill human needs and desires, and then that morality requires that such a being will that *everybody* including himself, not everybody *except* himself, do their share of the work of making sure that adequate human skills have been developed to fulfill human needs. Again, Kant's argument would work by applying both the principle of general rationality which underlies hypothetical imperatives and the specifically moral principle of pure practical reason: someone who applied only the former principle might be willing to have only others work in order to fulfill his own needs (although since other people do not like freeloaders, he would have to be very clever in order to get away with this for very long), but an agent committed to the moral value of universal law will insist that everyone including himself contribute to the development of human talents that is necessary to fulfill human needs and desires.

The only obvious flaw in Kant's conception of this duty is the suggestion that everyone must develop *all* of his or her natural talents or predispositions to skill. The combination of the general canon of rationality that adequate means to desired ends be available and the moral principle that everyone should make an equal contribution to this goal does not require that everyone develop all of their talents or that everyone develop the same talents; it requires only that everyone work together to make sure that sufficient human skills be collectively developed to make possible the collective satisfaction of human ends. This is quite compatible with each person developing only some of their possible skills and with different people developing different skills. Indeed, as we have known since Adam Smith's *Wealth of Nations* (1776) if not before, the end of collectively satisfying human needs is probably *best* met if different people develop different skills and each develops only some of their potential skills. Moreover, any one person's developing *all* of her potential skills is at least empirically if not logically impossible: the perfection of many human skills requires so much practice and has such specific effects on the human body and mind that there are many skills that simply cannot be conjointly developed by one person. Thus, even though one person might at a certain age have equal potential to become a ballet dancer or a defensive tackle, it is not physically possible for him subsequently to cultivate both of those talents: each develops the human body in ways different from and incompatible with the other. Kant should have argued only that each person must will the less determinate maxim of developing *some* talents necessary to satisfy human ends because only *that* maxim can be willed as a universal law by a prudent and moral rational being.

Kant's second discussion of the duty to cultivate some of one's talents, after the statement of FEI, is brief. He says that it is not enough that our actions not 'conflict' with the humanity in our own person, but they must also 'harmonize' with it. He then says that while it would be consistent with the mere 'preservation' of humanity (the humanity in our person) to neglect the 'predispositions to greater perfection that belong to the ends of nature in our regard to the humanity in our subject,' this would not be consistent with the 'furtherance' or 'promotion' of this humanity as an end in itself (4:430). This makes it sound as if Kant's position is some sort of naturalistic teleological perfectionism, according to which it is *our* duty to cultivate our predispositions to various skills because *nature* has placed them in us and thereby somehow obliged us to develop them. As already noted, although Kant does sometimes lapse into this language, it seems inconsistent with the third *Critique*'s strictly regulative reconstruction of teleology for him to rely upon it for fundamental principles of morality as well as of natural science. Instead, what he should have said here is that our duty toward humanity or rational being includes not only the duty not to destroy, injure, or restrict it in ourselves or others, but also the duty to promote the realization of the particular ends that we and others set for ourselves in the free exercise of our humanity, ends which may be attractive to the individuals whose ends they are out of mere inclination, but ends which become ends for all because they have been freely chosen in accordance with moral law in the exercise of our humanity. The cultivation of our own talents is then the necessary means to the realization of these necessary ends. What Kant also does not say but should have is that because we have not only the negative duty to preserve humanity whether in ourselves or others but also the positive duty to promote the realization of the particular ends set through the exercise of humanity in others as well as in ourselves, we should also have the duty not merely to develop our own talents but also to assist others in the development of theirs. This would be the basis for a duty to contribute to or to facilitate the education of others, indeed not just of our own children (a duty that Kant does recognize in the *Metaphysics of Morals*, 'Doctrine of Right,' §29, 6:281), but also of others who need education and whom we may be in a position to assist in fulfilling this need, whether it be by becoming a teacher, paying taxes for public education, making charitable contributions to private schools, colleges, and universities, or other suitable means.

  d. The Duty of Beneficence. Kant's final example is a case of imperfect duty toward others, commonly called the duty of beneficence or mutual aid. It is reasonably called by both names, for in the discussion of this duty after the statement of FUL/FLN, Kant treats it as the duty to help others who 'have to struggle with great hardships' (4:423), thus as a duty of mutual aid or assistance, while in his second discussion of it after the statement of FEI, he treats it as a more general duty to assist others in the pursuit of their own happiness through the realization of their own ends (4:430), thus as a more general duty of beneficence. Kant's term for 'hardship' is *Mühseligkeit*, and his term for happiness is *Glückseligkeit*, literally being 'blessed with trouble' and 'blessed with good fortune.' He might have been led by the structural similarity of these terms to regard them as antonyms, and thus to think that he has simply given a negative and a positive description of the same duty. But there would seem to be a difference between a duty to help only those who are in some situation of real difficulty or crisis, and a duty to help others realize particular ends that would no doubt add to their happiness but who are nevertheless already in pretty good circumstances. In fact, Kant's arguments support the more rather than less general duty, so it may be better to call this fourth duty by the more encompassing name, the duty of beneficence. However, as we will subsequently discuss, this duty is an imperfect duty, that is, we have to use judgment in deciding how much we have to do in order to fulfill it while also fulfilling our other duties and pursuing our own legitimate ends, and it may be useful (if unintentional) of Kant to use two different descriptions of it to remind us that we will face a spectrum of needs and wants in others, ranging from situations of real desperation where we have little choice but to help another to situations of milder need where we have more choice.

In both cases, Kant's explanations of this fourth duty are quite brief. In his first discussion of the example, which we can consider as an attempt to derive the narrower duty of mutual aid rather than the broader duty of beneficence from FUL/FLN, Kant argues that while the person for whom things are going well might think that it is permissible for him to refrain from helping others, because after all there is no contradiction in a world in which people do not help each other, nevertheless it is impossible for him 'to **will** that such a principle should be universally valid as a law of nature.' For, Kant continues, 'a will that decided this would conflict with itself, since the case could sometimes arise where he needs the love and sympathy of others but where, through such a law of nature, arisen from his own will, he would have robbed himself of all hope for the assistance for which he wishes' (4:423). The argument seems to be that although there is no conflict between the maxim to refrain from helping others and the world that results from the universalization of that maxim, the universalization of the maxim nevertheless violates the conditions of rational willing because by means of it the will would be depriving itself of what might be the only available means to the satisfaction of its ends in circumstances that are readily imaginable and, even if not currently present, quite likely to arise in any normal human life. (Again, of course, in the derivation of particular duties we may, indeed must take account of basic features of actual human existence.) This does seem to be an argument that any rational person capable of looking beyond the good fortune of the present moment should take seriously. The problem is that it seems to be an argument that any merely *prudent* person should consider; that is, it looks as if in this case considering what the consequences of the universalization of one's proposed maxim would be and realizing that one should not adopt that maxim are driven solely by prudence, by the concern that the universalization of this maxim would have untoward consequences for oneself.

Barbara Herman has argued that a prudential interpretation of this argument can be avoided by thinking of the rational will as driven to concern itself with the future availability of means for its own ends not by a mere desire for happiness, that is, by prudence, but rather by a concern to maintain the conditions necessary for its future existence and ability to operate as a rational will, a concern that is in turn grounded in the recognition of its unconditional value as a rational will, which is the basis of morality.[18] We could adapt this proposal to the approach taken in this book by saying that it is a concern for the future efficacy of one's freedom rather than just one's existence as a rational being that is the source of this duty. It would also be close to the spirit of the arguments that we have found in the previous examples to suggest that where Kant means for moral as opposed to merely prudential considerations to come into his argument is in the step of universalization itself. For while mere prudence may require us to think about how we would fare in circumstances different from our present ones, mere prudence does not require us to think about how we would fare if our maxim were universalized, for in the real world as we know it empirically our own maxims do not always lead by causal processes to their own universalization. Rather, it is only the principle of morality, that is, the categorical imperative, that requires us to consider how things would be, including how things would go for ourselves, if our maxims were to be universalized. In this case, prudence might lead us to think we could satisfy our own future needs even if we do not help others when we might as long as we manage to hide our own maxims from others and can therefore count on their good will; but morality will not allow us to make an exception of ourselves, and thus requires us to ask ourselves if we could accept a world in which everyone acts on the maxim we are proposing for ourselves. Then even if we are concerned merely with our future happiness, not with our continued existence as valuable rational beings, the generalization of our maxims that is demanded only by morality will tell us that we cannot make it our policy always to refrain from helping others.

That something like this is what Kant has in mind is confirmed by his derivation of the duty of beneficence toward others from the requirement that maxims be fit to be universal laws in the 'Doctrine of Virtue' in the later *Metaphysics of Morals* – a fact that is quite striking since, as Allen Wood has pointed out, that is the *only* place in that work where Kant derives a positive duty from the requirement of universalizability rather than directly from the absolute value of humanity as an end in itself.[19] In this work, Kant is initially entirely hostile to the idea that one could have any duty toward *one's own* happiness, since, he claims, that is something we all naturally desire, and duty concerns only that which we do *not* naturally desire but have to compel ourselves or be compelled to fulfill (Introduction, section IV, 6:386); in this mood, Kant grudgingly admits only that since being unhappy, or being in 'adversity, pain, and want,' is a great temptation 'to violate one's duty,' one may have an *indirect* duty to secure one's own happiness in order to remove temptation to violate *other* duties (Introduction, section V.B, 6:388). However, when Kant subsequently discusses the 'duty of love toward other human beings,' which is at the core of our positive duties toward others, he makes the following argument:

> In accordance with the ethical law of perfection 'love your neighbor as yourself,' the maxim of benevolence (practical love of human beings) is a duty of all human beings toward one another, whether or not one finds them worthy of love. – For, every morally practical relation to human beings is a relation among them represented by pure reason, that is, a relation of free actions in accordance with maxims that qualify for a giving of universal law and so cannot be selfish. I want everyone else to be benevolent

toward me; hence I ought also to be benevolent toward everyone else. But since all **others** with the exception of myself would not be **all**, so that the maxim would not have within it the universality of a law, which is still necessary for imposing obligation, the law making benevolence a duty will include myself, as an object of benevolence, in the command of practical reason. This does not mean that I am thereby under an obligation to love myself (for this happens unavoidably, apart from any command, so there is no obligation to it); it means instead that lawgiving reason, which includes the whole species (and so myself as well) in its idea of humanity as such, includes me as giving universal law along with all others in the duty of mutual benevolence, in accordance with the principle of equality, and **permits** you to be benevolent toward yourself on the condition of your being beneficent toward every other as well. (*MM*, 'Doctrine of Virtue,' §27, 6:450–1)

One of Kant's premises in this discussion, that no one can have a duty toward their own happiness because everyone naturally desires that, is patently wrong, at least if one thinks about long-term happiness: people often want momentary pleasures that will be deleterious to their long-term happiness, and may be able to refrain from the short-term indulgence only if they think of their long-term happiness as a duty. But that mistake does not undermine his present argument, which is that *morality*'s requirement of universalizability – which is essentially the requirement that you treat everybody equally, not claiming privileges for yourself that you are not willing to extend to others (the 'principle of equality' as Kant calls it here) – means that you cannot rightfully claim benevolence toward yourself if you are not willing to be benevolent toward others. Your desire for benevolence toward yourself may be entirely natural, but to expect it from others becomes morally permissible only if you are willing to extend it to others. This is not a prudential argument, but a moral argument.[20]

So in the end we can find a non-prudential argument from FUL/FLN to the duty of beneficence. But Kant's derivation of this duty from the value of humanity as an end in itself is more straightforward. Here he simply says that although one's own happiness is merely 'an end of nature that all human beings have,' we nevertheless have a duty to advance the happiness of others because 'positive agreement with **humanity as an end in itself**' requires that 'everyone try, as far as he can, to further the ends of others.' This is because 'the ends of the subject, which is an end in itself, must, if that representation is to have its **full** effect on me, also be as far as possible **my** ends' (*G*, 4:430). That is to say, since humanity is the power freely to set and pursue one's own ends, what it is to make humanity an end in itself is not merely to refrain from destroying or injuring that power, but also to assist people, who are 'subjects' or instances of humanity as much as oneself, in realizing their freely chosen ends. And since happiness is simply what results from the realization of ends, by means of this argument one has a duty to assist others in the realization of their happiness, even though it is not their mere desire for happiness that creates this duty but rather the value of their humanity which is as it were transmitted to their free choice of particular ends. Moreover, although Kant is reluctant to acknowledge it, this argument creates a direct rather than indirect duty toward one's own happiness, since after all humanity is present in one's own person as much as in that of any other.

It may now seem as if Kant has provided two entirely different and unrelated arguments for the duty of beneficence. However, it would seem better to think of the derivation of this duty from the absolute value of humanity as providing the rationale for its derivation from the requirement of acting only on universalizable maxims. That is, the requirement that one not demand privileges for oneself that one is not prepared to extend to others, which is expressed in the requirement of universalizability, does not come out of nowhere or even out of some purely abstract conception of rationality as universal; it arises from the assumption that humanity is absolutely valuable and equally valuable wherever it occurs, whether in oneself or others. In the end, then, the relation among Kant's two discussions of the four examples of duty confirms his suggestion that the unconditional value of humanity is the 'ground of a possible categorical imperative' understood as the requirement for the universalizability of maxims (4:428).

This largely completes our exposition of Kant's examples. However, Kant's qualification in his second discussion of the duty of beneficence that one has a duty to promote the happiness of others 'as far as possible' reminds us of a distinction that we mentioned at the outset of this section but did not extensively discuss, namely the distinction between perfect duties, which are 'strict,' and imperfect duties, which we apparently need to fulfill only 'as far as

possible.' Before we conclude this chapter by discussing some objections to Kant's categorical imperative, let us consider this distinction
somewhat further.

5. PERFECT AND IMPERFECT DUTIES

At the end of the first exposition of his four examples of duty, Kant
says that it is easy to see that some actions that would be violations
of duty, namely duties of the first two types discussed, would be such
'that their maxim cannot even be **thought** as a universal law of nature
without contradiction,' while in violations of duties like those in the
third and fourth examples, 'this inner impossibility is not to be
found, but it is still impossible to **will** that their maxim be elevated
to the universality of a law of nature, because such a will would contradict itself' (4:424). That is, it would be strictly impossible to act
on a maxim like that of making false promises to get out of financial
troubles in a world in which that maxim was universalized because
there would be no acceptance of promises in such a world, while
acting on a maxim like that of indifference toward the needs of
others would not be impossible in a world in which that maxim were
universalized, but would be incompatible with the general conditions for being both a prudential and a moral will. Referring back to
his original statement that his own division of duties will reflect the
common distinction between perfect and imperfect duties (4:421),
Kant then says that it is obvious that duties of the first kind correspond to 'strict or narrow (unremitting) duty,' while those of the
second type correspond with 'wide (meritorious) duty'; since these
two types of duty exhaust the possibilities, Kant can be confident
that 'through these examples . . . all duties have been fully set forth
in their dependence on [his] single principle' (4:424). In his discussion of the duty of beneficence after FEI Kant also repeats the suggestion that this is a 'meritorious duty,' that is, one the fulfillment of
which is somehow especially worthy of commendation (4:430). In
his footnote to the original mention of the distinction between
perfect and imperfect duties Kant explained the distinction between
strict, narrow, and unremitting duties and wide duties as that
between duties that permit no exception for the sake of inclination
and those that apparently do, and it would seem that he means that
the fulfillment of an imperfect or wide duty is especially meritorious
because one is never strictly speaking obliged to fulfill such a duty,

but could always allow oneself an exception from doing so on the basis of inclination.

This seems a surprising thing for a supposedly strict moralist like Kant to say, which is one point that needs discussion. Another issue here concerns the relation between Kant's distinction between perfect and imperfect duties and the traditional version of this distinction, which goes back to such natural law theorists as Hugo Grotius (1583–1645) and Samuel Pufendorf (1632–94). For them, the distinction was one between duties that are 'perfect' in the sense of being enforceable by or on behalf of the person or persons to whom they are owed and duties that are not – as Pufendorf put it, duties the fulfillment of which can be 'extorted by Force, or by the Rigor of Law,' and duties the fulfillment of which cannot be so 'extorted.'[21] What is the connection between this definition of the distinction and Kant's?

We can address both of these issues by looking at the way Kant interprets the distinction in the later *Metaphysics of Morals*. Here Kant draws a distinction between duties that proscribe or prescribe specific *actions*, such as the proscription of false promises or the prescription of the repayment of debts, and duties that prescribe *ends*, such as the happiness of others or one's own physical or mental perfection, but which cannot prescribe all of the specific actions by means of which those ends might be realized. Kant calls these duties of 'narrow obligation' and 'wide obligation' respectively: duties of narrow obligation prescribe or proscribe specific types of actions, but duties of wide obligation prescribe only general ends that might be realized through a variety of means (*MM*, 'Doctrine of Virtue,' Introduction, section VII, 6:390). This is the basis for his distinction between duties of right, which may be enforced by the external disincentives provided by law (punishments), and ethical duties or duties of virtue, which may not be enforced by law but only by the internal motivation of respect for the moral law as such. As we have already seen, the duties that prescribe or proscribe specific actions are not as simple as they might at first seem: the fact that the moral law is applied to maxims rather than directly to actions means that actions such as false promises are not necessarily proscribed in all circumstances, but only when they would be performed for certain specific reasons and motivations. The law takes account of this by making certain intentions elements of a crime or exculpatory factors. It should also be noted that not all prescriptions or proscriptions of particular types of actions performed under particular maxims are enforceable by law. For although a certain degree of specificity is a *necessary* condition for legal enforcement – the law cannot punish you for failing to perform one type of action that might fulfill a general end on one occasion, when you could always argue that you have performed or intended to perform different types of actions that would satisfy that general duty on other occasions – there are certain types of actions that, although they are specific enough, may harm only the agent himself and which others, that is to say, the public acting through the law, do not have the standing or right to enforce or punish. For example, no one else may have the right to prevent a suicide or punish an attempted (but failed) suicide that would harm no one but the suicide himself (of course, the law has not always recognized this constraint). As other writers of the period put it, a perfect duty that includes the right to legal prevention or punishment also requires a 'moral capacity' or 'title' on the part of those who would enforce the right.[22] Kant does not explicitly discuss this condition, but he tacitly employs it for his own distinction between duties of right and duties of virtue by including under the former only those duties that are coercively enforceable and including among the latter both specific duties that no one has the moral right to enforce as well as the general duties to adopt an end that are not even candidates for legal enforcement because they are not specific enough. Thus Kant himself classified the duty not to commit suicide, a perfect duty toward oneself, as a duty of virtue rather than a duty of right, because no one else has the moral standing to enforce that duty.

So the connection between Kant's distinction between perfect and imperfect duties and the traditional one is that Kant's distinction between the prescription or proscription of specific types of actions performed for specific reasons and the prescription of more general ends is a necessary although not sufficient condition for the traditional distinction between what may be legally enforced and what may not be. Kant's distinction between perfect duties as narrow prescriptions or proscriptions of actions and imperfect duties as broad prescriptions of ends that may be realized through many different actions also explains his remark in the *Groundwork* about exceptions, although it turns out that what he says there is misleading. There he suggested, as we saw, that one might simply allow oneself an exception to an imperfect duty out of inclination, and that, conversely, the fulfillment of an imperfect duty is meritorious (or as we might now say, supererogatory) because one fulfills it even though one *could* have allowed oneself an exception from doing so on the basis of mere inclination. This is not what Kant says in the *Metaphysics of Morals*. Here he says that

> If the law can command only the maxims of actions, not the actions themselves, that is a sign that it leaves room for play (*latitudo*) for the free power of choice in following this law (compliance), i.e., it cannot determine precisely how and to what extent the end that is at the same time duty is to be effected through action. – But a broad duty should not be understood as a permission for exceptions from the maxims of actions, but only for the restriction of one maxim of action by another (e.g., the restriction of the general love of neighbors by the love of parents). (*MM*, 'Doctrine of Virtue,' Introduction, section VII, 6:390)

Because an imperfect duty prescribes only a general end such as self-improvement or the happiness of others, it must leave the choice of particular means by which to realize such ends up to the judgment and preferences of particular individuals: the general end of self-improvement by itself cannot determine whether I should develop my potential to become a philosopher or a pianist, and the general end of helping others cannot determine whether I should help others by teaching them philosophy or working in a soup kitchen. A general end of helping others also cannot demand that I should help everyone in need, because that is impossible. Further, as Kant suggests, one way of fulfilling an imperfect duty may have to give way to another in particular circumstances: in circumstances where I cannot help both my neighbors and my parents, I may have the duty to do the latter rather than the former (though in some other circumstances it may be the reverse). Or it may not be possible to fulfill two different imperfect duties at the same time: thus I may have to decide whether it is more appropriate now to work on my own self-development than to be out helping others, or whether the latter is more pressing at the moment, and the general ends cannot settle this particular question for me. Moreover, although Kant does not say this here, there are circumstances in which a broad or imperfect duty to promote a general end may have to give way to a narrow or perfect obligation: thus, I cannot make a false promise to one person or refuse to pay back a debt that I owe in order to get money to give to charity. So one way of fulfilling an imperfect duty may be restricted by another way of fulfilling the same duty, one imperfect duty may be restricted by another, or fulfilling imperfect duty may be restricted by the demands of perfect duty: for all these reasons the general ends of imperfect duty cannot give rise to inflexible rules for their fulfillment, and judgments about the needs and circumstances of oneself and others are needed. For this reason, it must be possible to make exceptions to anything that would look like a *specific rule* for fulfilling the general ends of imperfect duty. But that does *not* mean that one can allow oneself an exception from the demands of imperfect duty *from mere inclination*: that I just do not feel like it now is not an acceptable reason for refusing to help someone else in need. And for that matter, there are plenty of circumstances that do not leave any room for judgment and preference even in fulfilling imperfect duties: thus, if someone is about to drown in front of me, and I know how to swim and rescue someone, and there is no one else drowning to whom I have a greater obligation, then in *those* circumstances I may indeed have an 'unremitting' duty to try to rescue that person, and will deserve severe censure or even punishment if I do not try, even if *in some other circumstances* I would not have the same duty.[23]

So this is Kant's distinction between perfect and imperfect duties properly understood. It seems to be an eminently sensible distinction, and the fact that his distinction between maxims that would be undermined by their own universalization and maxims such that they themselves would not be undermined by their own universalization but where our rational and moral will considered more generally would be can support this distinction seems a strong argument in favor of his conception of the categorical imperative. That said, however, we must now consider some common objections to Kant's categorical imperative.

6.   OBJECTIONS TO THE CATEGORICAL IMPERATIVE

Most objections to Kant's categorical imperative are actually objections to its first formulation, FUL/FLN. There does not seem to be much room for objection to Kant's requirement that humanity should always be treated as an end and never merely as a means except that it is high-sounding but vague; but Kant's detailed derivation of specific ethical duties to both ourselves and others in the 'Doctrine of Virtue' of the *Metaphysics of Morals* belies that objection. We do not have room here for a detailed discussion of those duties,[24] so let us concentrate on the objections to FUL/FLN. There are two main sorts of objections to FUL/FLN. The first is that it produces so many results that conflict with our common beliefs about what is morally permissible and impermissible that it cannot possibly be right. The other is that although it may successfully ground our perfect, typically negative duties such as the prohibition of false promises, it cannot ground imperfect, positive duties such as the duty of beneficence.

i. False Positives and Negatives

The first objection, more specifically, is that FUL/FLN yields so many false positives, that is, maxims that should be impermissible on any reasonable view of morality but that turn out to be permissible according to FUL/FLN, and false negatives, that is, maxims that should be permissible on any reasonable view of morality but that turn out to be impermissible according to FUL/FLN, that it cannot possibly be a correct expression of the real principle of morality.[25] Here are some typical examples that are supposed to yield such unwanted results. First, two that are supposed to yield false positives. Take a Nazi death-squad member whose maxim is to murder as many Jews as possible; ask him if he would be willing to have his maxim universalized, that is, for everyone to adopt the maxim of killing as many Jews as possible, and instead of finding himself in a contradiction he gleefully says 'Of course!' – his maxim is supposed to have passed the test of universalizability, but is clearly morally heinous to the highest degree. Or take a red-haired bank robber named Ignatz MacGillycuddy who wants to rob a bank northeast of his own house at 5 p.m. on a certain Thursday and then, let's say, to deposit the proceeds in his account at his own bank the next day.[26] He claims that his maxim is that a red-haired person named Ignatz MacGillycuddy should rob any bank that is open northeast of his house at 5 p.m. on any Thursday. When asked whether he could will the universalization of his maxim without undermining his own maxim and the end that he has in it, he answers 'Of course! After all, even if every red-haired person named Ignatz MacGillycuddy with banks northeast of their houses that are open at 5 p.m. on Thursdays should rob those banks, there just are not enough such people to bring down the whole banking system; so even if all such people do adopt my maxim, there will still be enough money in the bank I am going to rob on Thursday for me to get some loot to deposit in my own bank, which will still be in business on Friday and long after.' Yet bank-robbing under any circumstances, or under almost any circumstances but certainly in these circumstances, is surely wrong, even if MacGillycuddy can successfully universalize his maxim. Now for a case that is supposed to yield a false negative, take one that we have already considered: I make it my maxim to play tennis at 10 a.m. on Sundays, when most of the other players will be otherwise occupied and the courts will not be crowded. But when asked whether I could still make this my maxim even if it were universalized, that is, if everyone were to make it his or her maxim to play tennis on Sundays at 10 a.m., I realize that this would defeat my purpose of playing when the courts are least crowded. So I cannot will both my maxim and its universalization without the latter undermining the former, that is, my maxim fails FUL/FLN – but surely there is nothing morally impermissible with having the policy of playing tennis on Sunday mornings because that is when the courts will be least crowded. So once again FUL/FLN cannot be the proper expression of the fundamental principle of morality.

The first line of defense against such counterexamples is to argue that the maxims that have been ascribed to the agents in them, and which have either passed or failed the test of universalization when they should not have, are not the maxims on which those agents really propose to act and which they would admit to if they were at all honest with themselves or with us. Thus, it will be argued, the Nazi killer's real maxim is not simply that he should kill as many Jews as possible, but something more like 'Out of self-love I shall kill as many of my enemies as I like'; then when he is asked whether he could will the universalization of *that* maxim while continuing to act upon it himself, he will have to realize that he could not, because surely there are plenty of people (thank goodness) who will regard *him* as their enemy, and will be licensed to kill *him* and prevent him from killing his enemies. So his maxim would not pass the test of universalization after all. Or, in the case of Ignatz MacGillycuddy, if he were honest he would admit that his maxim is really something like 'Out of self-love I shall rob whatever banks I find it convenient or amusing or otherwise preferable to rob, or indeed get money in whatever way I find preferable regardless of the ownership rights or personal safety of other people'; and then when he was asked whether he could will both his own maxim and the universalization of that maxim, he would have to admit that the universalization of his maxim would quickly undermine the whole banking system and indeed the entire institution of property rights, so that it would indeed defeat his purpose in acting on that maxim in the first place. So his maxim would not pass the test of universalization after all. Conversely, the tennis player's real maxim should be something like 'Out of self-love, I will try to find a time to play tennis or enjoy my other avocations when the facilities are least crowded and it is otherwise convenient for me'; and there will surely be no contradiction between that maxim and its universalization, because in fact not everyone enjoys the same avocations, finds the same times for them convenient, and so on. And even if it does turn out that there is no particular time when the courts are less crowded than at all other times, the person will still have the possibility of modifying his policy of playing only when there is the shortest wait, or of giving up that avocation altogether and finding something else to do – after all, the goal of playing tennis is an optional end, and the policy of always going to play when the courts are least crowded is only based on the principle of hypothetical imperatives, that is, of finding a sufficient means for an optional end, which is compatible with giving up the end if no adequate means to it can be found.[27]

Now it may be objected to this defense of Kant's principle that any particular action could be performed under an indefinite number of different maxims, and that the possibility of ascribing his 'real' or 'sincere' maxim to an agent on which this defense depends is undermined by this fact. How is an outside observer or judge supposed to determine whether the Nazi's real maxim is to kill Jews in particular or to kill his enemies, whoever they might happen to be? After all, Kant himself famously insisted that our real motives are often inscrutable to ourselves (4:407) – so how can we presume that one person's real motive and real maxim can be clear to anyone else? The answer to this objection is that in formulating FUL/FLN (or any of the other versions of the categorical imperative) Kant is not actually setting up a test for the moral evaluation of previously performed actions, to be used *ex post facto* in the moral equivalent of a courtroom; he is formulating a test by means of which ideal moral agents could test the moral status of their proposed actions *ex ante*, that is, he is setting up a standard for moral *deliberation* about duties and rights in general rather than for moral *appraisal* of particular performances; and in this case we could plausibly argue that conscientious ideal moral agents, who have all the time they need for deliberation, or whose deliberation does not take place in real time at all, should and would in fact evaluate a proposed action or type of action under *all* of the maxims that might plausibly and reasonably apply to it. So such a moral deliberator would not decide that an action is permissible just because it passes the universalization test when it is subsumed under the narrowest maxim that might apply to it; she would test it under broader maxims as well, and she would regard it as morally impermissible (or permissible) if it fails (or passes) the test of such broader maxims. Thus, while a real Nazi might protest that his maxim was only that he or everyone should kills Jews, not just any old enemies, an ideal moral deliberator would nevertheless realize that the Nazi's maxim was in fact just a narrow instance of the broader maxim to kill one's enemies, whoever they are, and would see that the latter maxim cannot be universalized.

This response still leaves room for the possibility that one and the same type of action may fail the test of the categorical imperative if performed for one reason, that is, with one maxim, but pass if performed with another – for example, making a false promise for one's own financial gain and out of the motive of self-love may fail the test, but making a false promise in order to save the life of an innocent person may pass the test. But this, as we saw earlier, is not really an objection to Kant's principle at all, but if anything a confirmation of it. For the law recognizes that the nature of the motive and reason of an action can make a crucial difference to its legality, for example when it distinguishes between criminal homicide (of course the vast majority of cases) and justifiable homicide (a much smaller number of cases) on the basis of the agent's beliefs and motives (did he really believe that his own life or that of another innocent person was under an unjustifiable attack, or is that just a self-serving pretense?). So too morality in general should recognize such a distinction, even when the duty in question is not a legally enforceable one: although it may be best that there be no legal penalties for breaking lunch-dates, there is still a moral difference between breaking a date, even without advance notice, because your favorite store just announced a sale and you suddenly decided you would rather go shopping instead of keeping your date, and breaking it because your child has just been rushed to the hospital and you need to be at her side. A moral theory that did *not* recognize such differences in circumstances and motivations – in other words, in maxims – and that instead treated all outwardly similar actions the same would be seriously deficient.

ii. Negative and Positive Duties

A different objection that has been urged against FUL/FLN is that although this formula of the categorical imperative can successfully yield negative duties, that is, prohibitions such as the prohibition against false promises out of self-love, it does not yield the imperfect, positive duties such as the duty of beneficence. This is because the impermissibility of adopting one maxim allegedly does not yield the necessity of acting on any other maxim. Thus, for example, Allen Wood argues that 'From the mere fact that we may *not* adopt some specific principle as a norm,' for example the principle never to help others in need, 'it can never follow directly that we *must* adopt some other normative principle,' such as the principle 'To help some others sometimes.'[28]   But this seems wrong: just as the falsity of one statement implies the truth of its contradictory, e.g. 'It is false that it is raining today' implies 'It is true that it is not raining today,' so it would seem that the impermissibility of adopting one maxim does imply the necessity of adopting its contradictory, thus the impermissibility of the maxim of never helping anyone does imply the necessity of the maxim of helping somebody sometime. However, even if this is right, there is still a problem here, namely that such a necessity as that of having to help somebody sometime falls short of what Kant has in mind as the positive duty of beneficence. The problem is not that such a general duty does not imply anything very particular, such as donating so many dollars every month to Oxfam or Save the Children; Kant does not intend the imperfect duty of beneficence to mechanically imply anything as precise as that, nor should he – how any specific person should fulfill the duty of beneficence depends upon all sorts of factors about her circumstances, resources, other obligations, and so on that could not be captured by any simple rule. The problem is rather that even Kant's properly general statements of the duty of beneficence are more demanding than the minimal obligation to help someone sometime: thus in his second statement of the duty of beneficence, which is supposed to describe the same duty that also follows from FUL/FLN, Kant says, as we saw earlier, that one must try to help others 'as far as he can' or 'as far as possible' (4:430), and, although this is still general rather than specific, it is surely more demanding than just 'help someone sometime.' The question is then whether Kant can derive this stronger result from the impermissibility of adopting the maxim 'Never help anyone' when tested by FUL/FLN.

We might be able to answer this problem by returning to the version of the derivation of the duty of beneficence from the requirement of universalizability that Kant gave in the *Metaphysics of Morals*. There, it will be recalled, Kant argued that the maxim of seeking one's own happiness, which would include within it as a matter of general rationality the desire for help from other people in realizing this end, is only moral if it is generalized into a policy of promoting the happiness of everyone by help from anyone, including oneself. If we were to use the principle that whoever wills the end should as a matter of rationality also will *adequate* means in order to make one's own maxim more precise and honest here, it might then be to seek one's own happiness with *as much* help from others as they could reasonably be expected to provide given their own resources, needs, other obligations, and so on. The universalization of *this* maxim, which is what morality demands, would then be something like that everyone should help everyone else realize their happiness as much as they can, given their own circumstances, resources, other obligations, and so on – that is to say, the maxim to help others 'as far as one can' or 'as far as possible.' If this is right, then FUL/FLN does yield as demanding a positive duty of beneficence as an argument from FEI would, and as demanding a duty of beneficence as anyone could want. Of course, even this argument would still not yield a duty to help *everyone* else *all* the time, that is, the extreme opposite of the maxim of never helping anyone, but neither Kant nor anyone else in his right mind wants to argue for a duty like that, because no human being could fulfill that demand in any effective way.

No doubt there are many other objections to the categorical imperative that need to be addressed. But here we could only make a start on this project, for now we must at last turn to the question of whether Kant can show that the categorical imperative that he has derived from the general idea of a free and rational being is actually possible for and binding upon us human beings, constituted as we actually are. This is the project of Section III of the *Groundwork*.

Study Questions
1. What is wrong with an empirical method of moral philosophy? Does Kant have a genuine alternative to it?
2. Can Kant successfully distinguish between hypothetical and categorical imperatives by saying that the former depend on ends and the latter do not? If not, is there another way for him to make this distinction?
3. What is a maxim?
4. What is the relation between Kant's derivation of FUL in Section II from the mere concept of a categorical imperative and his derivation of it in Section I from the exclusion of inclination from the motivation for duty?
5. What is the difference between a contradiction in conception and a contradiction with the rational will in the universalization of a maxim?
6. In what way is FEI the ground of the possibility of the categorical imperative understood as FUL/FLN?
7. What does Kant mean by the 'realm of ends,' and why should that be the ultimate object of morality?
8. Are any of Kant's derivations of specific duties from his various formulations of the categorical imperative persuasive? If so, which are most convincing?
9. Does Kant's category of 'imperfect duty' undermine the universality of moral principles?
10. Do we need to be able to discover the specific maxim on which an actual agent is acting in order successfully to use FUL/FLN as a moral principle in deliberation? in order to use the other versions of the categorical imperative as principles of deliberation?
11. How many different formulations of the categorical imperative does Kant use, and what is the relation among them?
12. Does Kant have a good way of arguing that he has identified the most fundamental principle of morality?

CHAPTER 6

READING THE TEXT: SECTION III.
THE CATEGORICAL IMPERATIVE APPLIES TO US

1. DOES THE CATEGORICAL IMPERATIVE APPLY TO US?

Throughout Section II of the *Groundwork*, Kant insisted that he was there deriving the categorical imperative from the pure concept of a rational will, and that only subsequently would he prove that this imperative applies to us human beings (e.g., 4:425, 431–2, 445). In fact, his presentation of the fundamental principle of morality *as* a categorical imperative, that is, a constraint upon agents who also have inclinations to do otherwise than what morality commands, as well as his illustrations of the types of duties that can be derived from the categorical imperative, both assumed certain key facts about human nature as contrasted to rational being in general, but as far as the principle of morality itself is concerned these parts of Kant's argument can be said to have presupposed rather than proved that the fundamental principle of morality that is valid for rational beings as such actually applies to and therefore binds us human beings. As far as the general principle is concerned, then, Kant's summary of what he accomplished in Section II and what remains to be done in Section III seems right:

> This section, like the first, was merely analytical. Now that moral-ity is no phantom of the brain, which follows if the categorical imperative and with it the autonomy of the will is true and as an *a priori* principle absolutely necessary demands a **possible syn-thetic use of pure practical reason**, which however we may not venture without preceding it with a **critique** of this faculty of reason itself, the chief features of which that are adequate for our purposes have to be exhibited in the final section. (4:445–6)

What Kant means by this is that the principle of morality that has been shown to follow from the concept of pure rational willing by analysis now has to be shown to apply to us, in the form of the categorical imperative, by a critique or examination of our own faculty of reason that will show it to include *pure* practical reason. Indeed, as Kant suggests several times in Section III, this critique must show not just that our reason includes pure practical reason but that pure practical reason expresses our 'authentic self' (4:458, 461), so that the principle of pure practical reason is more expressive of our real identity than the merely instrumental principles of ordinary practical reason, i.e., hypothetical imperatives that prescribe the means to ends that are not themselves determined by pure practical reason.

However, proving that 'morality is no phantom of the brain' could mean several different things. One thing it could require is proving that we are *capable* of acting as morality requires, so that being moral is not an *impossible* ideal for us. The other thing it could mean is that it must still be shown that morality *is* an obligatory norm for us, so that being moral is not an *irrelevant* ideal for us. Given Kant's exposition in Section II, we might expect that he would first attempt to prove the latter, that is, that the moral principle is really obligatory for us, and only subsequently attempt to prove the former, that we are in fact free to live up to this principle. However, this is not in fact how Kant proceeds in Section III. Rather, the main thrust of the section is a single argument, drawing on Kant's metaphysics, that, contrary to appearances, at the deepest level of our reality we really are purely rational agents who are not merely *under an obligation to act in accordance with the moral law* and also *free to do so if we so choose* but actually *cannot do otherwise than act in accordance with the moral law*. This argument entirely sidesteps the necessity of providing a purely normative argument that we *ought* to act in accordance with the moral law. It is also seriously problematic, however. In the end, while the metaphysics of Section III may advance beyond Section II in providing a reason for thinking that we are *capable* of acting in accordance with morality, it may not succeed in improving on Section II's suggestion that we *ought* to act in accordance with the moral law because there is a unique dignity in the autonomy that we achieve by so doing.

Some of Kant's own remarks about his aims in Section III may deflect our attention from this problem. At one point he characterizes his goal as resolving a 'dialectic of reason' that arises because the freedom of the will 'seems to stand in contradiction with natural necessity' (4:455), and thus the latter, that is, that subjection of all of nature including ourselves as creatures in nature to deterministic scientific laws, seems to contradict the assumption that we are always *capable* of acting in accordance with the categorical imperative, that is, free to do what it demands of us no matter what our upbringing, prior conduct, and so on might predict we will do. Such a dialectic would be resolved by showing how it is possible for us to have a free will even though from a scientific point of view our behavior is explicable and predictable in accordance with laws of nature. This would suggest that in Section III Kant is only trying to prove that the moral law *can* apply to us, because we are *capable* of acting in accordance with it, but not trying to prove that it *should* or *must* apply to us. Likewise, when at the end of Section III Kant announces that he has finally answered the question that was left open in Section II, namely, 'How is a categorical imperative possible?', by showing that our freedom, which is itself *presupposed* 'for the **practical use** of reason, i.e., for the conviction of the **validity of this imperative**,' is itself *possible* (4:461), this might suggest that all that had to be proven in Section III was that it is *possible* for us to act in accordance with this norm, not the norm itself.

However, if we think back to Kant's earlier discussion of the possibility of imperatives (4:417–20), we will recall that Kant thought there was no problem about explaining the possibility of *hypothetical* imperatives because in their case the *reason for* complying with them was *given* by mere inclination, and that in order to explain the *further* fact that in order to gratify our inclinations we are willing to conform to hypothetical imperatives all we had to do was realize that the principle 'Whoever wills the end wills the means' is analytically true of any rational will. This suggests that in order to answer the question 'How is the *categorical* imperative possible?' *both* the reason for as well as the possibility of complying with it must be demonstrated, that is, both the normative question of *why* we *should* comply with the categorical imperative as well as the factual question of *how* we *can* comply with it still must be answered. In this case, Section III would have to show both why the categorical imperative is an unconditional norm for us human beings as well as how it is possible for us to act in accordance with its unremitting demands in spite of what a naturalistic and deterministic conception of our behavior – which is itself a necessary part of science – might suggest.

As already suggested, however, the heart of Section III is actually a metaphysical argument that we necessarily *do* act in accordance with the categorical imperative, which would show in one fell swoop both that we must act in accordance with this law and that it is possible for us to act in accordance with it, since actuality implies possibility. However, we will also see that Kant backs off from this problematic argument, not only in all his later writings on moral philosophy, but even before the end of Section III of the *Groundwork* itself. He will there treat his metaphysical argument as if it had been intended to prove only the possibility of our acting in accordance with the categorical imperative. But that means that Kant will have given up on attempting to prove by metaphysical means the synthetic proposition that the categorical imperative is our most fundamental obligation, and that Section III in the end has nothing to add to Section II's appeal to our sense of dignity to motivate us to accept our obligation to live up to the categorical imperative.

2. THE TASK FOR SECTION III

Kant begins Section III with a restatement of what has been demonstrated in Section II that is both illuminating and confusing. It is illuminating because it is more explicit than was Section II that the connection between freedom and the moral law is the foundation of his entire argument in the *Groundwork*. It is confusing, however, because it also claims that the connection between freedom and thus the moral law, on the one hand, and even the pure concept of a rational being, on the other, is synthetic, although Section II had led us to believe that this connection is analytic, and that only the connection between the pure concept of a rational being and everything that it entails with *us* is synthetic and remains to be proven. That does remain to be proven, to be sure, and we still have to see how that connection is supposed to be proven; but now we will also have to see if we can make any sense of the claim that even the connection between freedom and the pure concept of a rational being is synthetic, or if that is just a misstatement on Kant's part.

Kant begins Section III with a contrast between 'negative' and 'positive' definitions of freedom. He first defines will as 'a kind of causality of living beings insofar as they are rational,' and then gives the negative definition that freedom is the 'quality of this causality in which it can be efficacious independently of foreign causes **determining** it'; this is in contrast to '**natural necessity**' as 'the quality of the will of all non-rational beings of being determined to activity through foreign causes' (4:446). The three key points to be noticed about this negative definition of freedom are that it says that the will is free insofar as it *can* be determined independently of foreign causes, not that it is free only if it *is* or *must* be so determined; that it locates freedom in the possibility of not being *determined* by foreign causes, but does not exclude all possible *influence* of foreign causes; and that it is entirely open-ended about what counts as a foreign cause, so open-ended, indeed, as we shall next see, that anything except determination of the will by itself alone, or by its own mere form, will not count as a realization of the potential freedom of the will. With regard to these three points, we will have to ask whether Kant sticks to the idea that freedom is merely the possibility of the will being self-determined rather than being determined by foreign causes, what it could mean for the will to be self-determined rather than being determined by foreign causes, and what it would mean for the will not to be determined but still to be influenced by foreign causes.

The answers to some of these questions become clear as Kant next introduces the positive definition of the freedom of the will. Here he says that since the conception of the will is a conception of a kind of causality and any concept of causality 'brings with it that of **laws**,' freedom cannot be the independence of the will from laws altogether; rather, it must be the independence of the will from determination in accordance with 'laws of nature' but its determination 'in accordance with immutable laws of a special kind.' Thus, the will cannot be free *merely* in the negative sense; it must also be free in the positive sense.[1] Specifically, while 'natural necessity was a heteronomy of efficient causes,' the freedom of the will in positive terms can be nothing 'other than autonomy, i.e., the quality of the will of being a law itself.' But, Kant continues,

The proposition that the will is itself a law in all of its actions designates only the principle of acting in accordance with no other maxim than one that can also have itself as a universal law as its object. But that is precisely the [first] formula of the categorical imperative and the principle of morality: thus a free will and a will under moral laws are identical. (4:446–7)

So what it means in positive terms for the will to be a species of causality that like any other is governed by a law but in negative terms for it not to be governed by the law of any external causes or heteronomy is for it to act in accordance with the mere *form* of law, that is, to act only on universalizable maxims. Thus the will that is free in the positive sense is nothing other than the will that governs itself by the moral law. To be sure, the *content* of the maxims of such a will will have to be suggested by factors external to the pure form of the will as such – for example, the maxim that I should seek the help of others in realizing my own happiness is suggested by the *natural* facts that I desire happiness and that I cannot count on always being able to provide it for myself – and that is the sense in which factors foreign to or external to the free will can *influence* it; but the will that is free in a positive sense acts on such suggested maxims only if it can universalize them, and that is the sense in which it is not *determined* by such external factors but is determined only by its own law.

Thus far Kant's argument may be clearer than his exposition in *Groundwork* II because it is explicitly about freedom and we do not have to infer that it is about freedom through a definition of his concept of humanity as an end in itself. However, we should also note that the argument has a decidedly metaphysical character: Kant does not argue, as he did in his pre-*Groundwork* texts, that the 'negative' goal of freedom from determination by inclination can be *achieved* only through conforming one's actions to a moral law, thus making conformity to the moral law the means to the end of freedom; rather, Kant argues on the basis of a general concept of causality that if the free will is not to be determined by natural laws linking inclinations to actions then it must be determined by some other law, indeed self-determined by another law, and then infers the content of that law from that supposition. Without this reliance on the concept of causality, the present argument would not work. And indeed this argument could be considered controversial by Kant's own lights, for in the *Critique of Pure Reason* he suggests that freedom may consist in the capacity to *initiate* a law-governed sequence of causes and effects through an act that is not itself the effect of any cause and is thus apparently not governed by any law at all.[2] Perhaps what Kant now means to tell us is that his characterization of freedom in the first *Critique* was incomplete (after all, he was hardly offering a fully developed moral philosophy there),

and that a free act has to be understood as an act that is not determined to follow from a prior stimulus by a mere law of nature, but
rather must be determined by a self-given law, but which then initi-
ates a further series of consequences that can be explained in accordance with natural laws. But he hardly says so explicitly.

Be this as it may, Kant now makes an explicit claim that is,
however, also confusing: he says that although 'If the freedom of the
will is presupposed, then morality together with its principle follows
from the mere analysis of its concept,' but that 'this is always a synthetic proposition,' namely, 'that an absolutely good will is that,
whose maxim, considered as a universal law, can always contain
itself in itself, for that quality can never be found through analysis
of the concept of an absolutely good will' (4:447). This is confusing
because the argument of Section I of the *Groundwork* was precisely
that the analysis of the concept of an absolutely good will *does* lead
to the universal law formulation of the categorical imperative
through the assumption that the good will expresses itself in the
form of the willingness to heed the demands of duty. Maybe all that
Kant now has in mind in calling the connection between the good
will and the lawful character of the free will synthetic is that the condition of lawfulness necessary to achieve a good will expresses itself
as a *demand* and *constraint* only in the specifically human condition
of having inclinations that are not always compatible with the
requirements of a morally good will; but if that is what he means,
then that does not fit very well with what he appears to be trying to
do at this stage of Section III, namely summing up the analysis of
Section II before proving that it applies to *us* as human beings.

An alternative possibility is that he is saying that the connection
between the concept of a good will and a free will that governs itself
autonomously in conformity with the principle of universalizability
is synthetic because it depends upon the *normative proposition that
the preservation and promotion of freedom has unconditional value*:
this could be the synthetic premise for the further syllogism that
since the good will also has unconditional value, the good will must
consist in autonomy or the exercise of the free will in accordance
with the categorical imperative. This would reflect the structure
of Kant's pre-*Groundwork* arguments for the moral law as well as
the structure that we have ascribed to Section II in arguing that the
concept of humanity is equivalent to the concept of freedom in the
setting of one's ends and that the *value* of humanity so understood

must be considered to be a fundamental normative claim on which Kant's entire derivation of the categorical imperative is founded. For Kant to say now that the connection between the good will and the will under moral law is synthetic would be a way for him both to emphasize that the argument of Section II is really an argument about freedom and that it must rest on a normative proposition about the value of freedom. Such an interpretation would, to be sure, be in some tension with Kant's claim that the argument of Section II is analytic throughout, although it would not be in tension with his claims that Section II leaves open the question of whether all its propositions apply to *us*; there is thus no problem in continuing to assume that Section III is intended to demonstrate that. Such an interpretation would also remind us, however, that it was not clear in Section II exactly how the normative proposition that humanity is unconditionally valuable is supposed to be proved. If Kant's present claim that the connection between the good will and the moral law is synthetic is supposed to imply that the proposition that autonomy is unconditionally valuable is synthetic, then Section III would seem to be aimed at proving that proposition.

Another thing that we might have expected Kant to say here is not that the connection between the *good* will and a will under moral laws is synthetic but rather that the connection between the *free* will and the moral law is synthetic, that is, that a free will is not necessitated by its mere concept to act only on universalizable maxims, but rather that it is a free *choice* of the will whether to act only on universalizable maxims, thereby preserving and promoting humanity and freedom both in itself and in others, or to act on maxims that are not universalizable, thereby undermining freedom in itself and/or in others. We might have expected Kant to say this as an explication of his initial suggestion that freedom is that quality of the will by which it *can* determine itself independently of foreign causes, that is, causes other than the preservation of the freedom of the will as such, which seems to leave open the possibility that the free will *might not* determine itself in such a way, that it could use its freedom on one occasion to undermine the freedom of itself and others on other occasions. In his discussion of suicide, for example, Kant clearly recognized that it is unfortunately *possible* for the free will to choose that act, that is, while the free will must conform to the moral law if it wants to preserve and promote freedom, so that conformity to the moral law is a *normative* necessity, it is not under any metaphysical *necessity* of doing so. However, he does not use the concept of the synthetic to make that point here. Rather, he is blocked from making this point now by his premise that as a kind of causality that is not determined by external laws the freedom of the will *must* be determined by an internal law. We shall come back to this point in our discussion of the central argument of *Groundwork* III in the next section of this chapter.

But that is yet to come. First we must complete our discussion of the opening moves of Section III. Invoking his general claim that the subject and predicate of a synthetic proposition must always be linked by a 'third thing' (*Pure R*, A 155/B 194), Kant says that freedom positively understood is the third thing that connects the good will and the moral law, because, as he assumes, a free will is a good will and, as he has explicitly argued, a free will is a will under moral laws. What he next wants to argue is that a rational being in general is free and therefore subject to the moral law, and then that *we* are rational beings and therefore subject to the moral law. Proving the latter is of course the central point of *Groundwork* III. The next step toward this conclusion is therefore to prove that 'Freedom must be presupposed as a quality of the will of all rational beings' (4:447). The key step in the demonstration of this proposition is the assertion that

> Every being that cannot act except **under the idea of freedom** is just on that account really free from a practical point of view, i.e., that all the laws that are inseparably bound up with freedom hold for it just as if its will were also to be declared free in itself and in a way valid in theoretical philosophy. Now I assert: That we must necessarily lend the idea of freedom, under which alone it acts, to every rational being that has a will. For in such a being we conceive of a reason that is practical, i.e., has causality in respect to its objects. (4:448)

Kant's idea seems to be that to be rational requires being able to conceive of one's actions as determined *by* reason. In the theoretical case of simply making a judgment, that means that the rational being must be able to conceive of its judgments as being determined by its reason, that is, by the application of the rules and standards of its reason to its evidence, itself gathered in accordance with rational principles. A rational theoretical agent does not conceive of its judgments as forced upon it by any outside agency, including whatever stimulus from the external world that it happens to have; it conceives of itself as making its judgments by gathering and evaluating its evidence in accordance with its own principles. In other words, it conceives of itself as a free and autonomous cognizer, exercising its judgment in accordance with rules stemming from its own reason. The rational practical agent conceives of itself in the same way, that is, it does not conceive of itself as simply being moved to act by stimuli external to its will, but rather conceives of itself as acting on the basis of its evaluation of the stimuli influencing its will on the basis of its own principles of reason. In other words, the rational practical agent conceives of itself as acting freely and autonomously – otherwise, it could not conceive of its reason as the source of its practice or actions. 'It must conceive of itself as the authoress of its actions, independent from foreign influences, consequently as practical reason or as the will of a rational being it must be regarded as free of itself, i.e., its will can only be its own will under the idea of freedom' (4:448). For a being to conceive of its own reason as the source of its actions is for it to conceive of itself as free from external influences – freedom negatively understood – and as determined by the law of its own will – freedom positively conceived.

Thus Kant argues that freedom fully conceived, that is, conceived both negatively and positively, is necessarily connected to the very idea of a practical rational being, that is, a rational agent. Now he can approach the question of whether *we* are such beings, who must conceive of ourselves as free and thus by the prior argument linking freedom and the moral law as necessarily subject to that law. In his words, 'We have at last traced the determined concept of morality back to the idea of freedom; but we have not yet proved this to be something real in ourselves and in human nature' (4:448); the task is now to prove that freedom and therefore morality is something 'real in ourselves and in human nature.' Kant first dismisses the idea that we could establish that we are free and therefore ought to subject ourselves to this principle 'as rational being[s] in general' by any *interest*, for what he means here by an interest would simply be any inclination toward a reward promised by the moral law or an aversion to a punishment threatened by it, and to act merely out of such an inclination would not, by the prior analysis, be to act freely. He emphasizes this point by saying that insofar as we are to be free we cannot be motivated simply by a desire for happiness, even for happiness distributed in accordance with the moral law, for that would still be to act merely from inclination; we can take an interest in even such happiness only on the basis of a prior commitment to the moral law, which in that case would not be *based* on an interest in happiness but would *create* one (4:449–50). This is an allusion to the doctrine of the highest good that Kant had already alluded to in the *Critique of Pure Reason* and will develop in the *Critique of Practical Reason* and later works.[3] But since we cannot conceive of ourselves as attached to or obligated by the moral law through any mere interest, how are we to show that we are connected to it? Kant expresses this concern by worrying that 'in the idea of freedom we have merely presupposed the moral law, namely the principle of the autonomy of the will itself, and could not prove its reality and objective necessity for itself' (4:449), or that there might be a 'sort of circle here,' namely that 'In the order of efficient causes we assume ourselves to be free in order to think of ourselves as free in the order of ends under moral laws, [but that] we afterwards think of ourselves as subject to these laws because we have attributed freedom of the will to ourselves' (4:450). His worry is that although *if* we could prove ourselves to be free then we could, by the initial argument of this section, prove ourselves to be subject to the moral law, we *might* just be assuming that we are subject to the moral law and inferring that we are free *from* that. This would beg the question, for we would still not have proved that we are subject to the moral law. In order to avoid this danger, Kant's strategy now is to exploit the immediately preceding argument, that is, the proof that subjection to the autonomous law of its own will is necessarily connected to the *general concept* of a rational being, by proving that *we are* rational beings and are therefore both free and subject to the moral law. The structure of his argument will thus be to show that this preceding analysis actually applies to us. The connection between the general idea of rational agency and subjection to the moral law is supposed to be analytic, and the proof that this analysis applies to us synthetic. Whether this fits with Kant's previous claim that the connection between the good will and the moral law is actually synthetic may remain problematic, but the relation between analysis and synthesis at this stage of Kant's argument is clear.

3.   THE METAPHYSICAL PROOF OF SECTION III

Kant now says that there is 'one way out' of this circle open to us, namely to ask 'whether if we think of ourselves through freedom as *a priori* efficient causes we do not adopt another standpoint than if we represent ourselves as effects in accordance with our actions' (4:450). This signals that Kant will now appeal to his metaphysical doctrine of transcendental idealism in order to prove that we are rational agents, therefore both free yet subject to the moral law. The overall strategy of the proof he is about to offer is to demonstrate that we human beings really are rational agents that necessarily act in accordance with the laws of such agents, thus in accordance with the moral law. Such a proof, if successful, would entirely sidestep the necessity of directly arguing from some purely normative consideration that we *ought* to be obligated by the moral law as well as of arguing that it is *possible* for us to act in accordance with the moral law, because it would show on metaphysical grounds that we *do* act in accordance with that law. As we shall see, however, the argument is deeply problematic.

Maintaining the stance of Section I that the fundamental principles of morality and now, as it turns out, their presuppositions are matters of 'common rational cognition,' Kant first argues that even the 'commonest understanding' draws a distinction between how things appear to us and how they are in themselves. In his main works on theoretical philosophy, Kant argues for this distinction in a multitude of ways,[4] but here he appeals to a single fact: that we all recognize that in any ordinary cognition 'representations that come to us without our choice (such as those of the senses) do not allow us to cognize [their] objects otherwise than as they affect us, in which what they may be in themselves remains unknown to us'; thus we recognize that through such representations 'we can attain only cognition of **appearances**, never of **things in themselves**.' Or as he also puts it, from the distinction that anyone can recognize between 'representations that are given to us from elsewhere and with regard to which we are passive' and 'those that we produce entirely from ourselves and which prove our activity . . . it follows of itself that behind the appearances one must still concede something else, that is not appearance, namely the things in themselves' (4:450–1). One might well ask why it should follow 'of itself' from the fact that we are 'affected' by external objects or that our representations of them are their *effects* upon us, which to be sure virtually nobody would deny, that the things that *cause* those effects *may* be different from the way in which we represent them and therefore unknown, let alone, as Kant actually seems to go on to assume, that they *must* be different and known to be different from the way they appear to us. This inference seems unmotivated. Kant must be deriving it from the assumption that causes and effects are logically distinct from one another, so that the properties of the cause cannot be inferred from the properties of the effect. This assumption was the premise for Hume's argument that causal connections cannot be known by reason,[5] and it was adopted by Kant in his insistence that causal connections must be synthetic rather than analytic.[6] Now it should be noted that even if it is assumed that cause and effect are logically distinct from one another, in the sense that as far as any rules of logic are concerned either could exist without the other, that by itself implies only that the two are numerically distinct, not that they must be qualitatively distinct, i.e., that one cannot infer anything about the properties of the cause from the properties of the effect. So Kant's inference from the mere fact that the representation of objects is a causal process to a necessary distinction between the properties represented in the effect and the actual properties of the cause may be unjustified from the outset. We shall see, however, that this is not the worst problem with his argument.

Let us continue with the argument. Kant's next step is to say that any reflective person will also recognize that the distinction between appearance and thing in itself also applies *to himself*, that is, that there is a difference between the way in which we appear to ourselves and the way in which we actually are:

> Even in his own case and especially on the basis of the knowledge of himself that the human being has through inner sensation he may not presume to cognize how he is in himself. For since he does not as it were create himself and he does not acquire his concept [of himself] *a priori*, but empirically, it is natural that he can draw information even about himself through inner sense and consequently only through the appearance of his nature and the way in which his consciousness is affected, while he nevertheless necessarily assumes that beyond this constitution of his own subject composed of mere appearances something else lies at its ground, namely his I, as it may be constituted in itself . . . (4:451)

Thus it must seem as if everything that we know about ourselves we know empirically and as a matter of mere appearance, so that we are completely ignorant about the underlying nature of ourselves. This would not seem to bode well for any metaphysical argument about our 'authentic self,' hence for any metaphysical proof that we really are rational agents bound by the moral law. The next step of Kant's argument, however, is designed to avert this danger and prove that we really are rational agents, with all that this entails. For what Kant now argues is that in fact we *do* have a way of knowing something about our real natures, about ourselves as we are in ourselves, and that what we can know by this means is precisely that we really are rational agents. He argues that

> The human being really finds in himself a faculty through which he is distinguished from all other things, indeed even from himself insofar as he is affected by objects, and that is **reason**. This, as pure self-activity . . . reveals such a pure spontaneity that it goes far beyond everything that sensibility can afford it . . . On this account a rational being itself, **as intelligence** . . . has two standpoints from which it can consider itself and cognize the laws of the use of its powers, consequently all its actions, **first**, insofar as it belongs to the world of the senses, under natural laws (heteronomy), **second**, as belonging to the intelligible world, under laws which, independent of nature, are not empirical but are grounded solely in reason. (4:452)

The laws that are independent from nature and grounded solely in reason are nothing but the moral law, so by this argument the human being as it is in itself, as opposed to how it merely appears to itself, is necessarily governed by the moral law. What applies to rational beings in general may not *appear* to apply to us, but does apply to us *as we really are*. This is the conclusion that would obviate the need to prove on normative grounds that the human being *ought* to be obligated by the moral law and, since actuality always implies possibility, would more than suffice to prove that we are *capable* of acting in accordance with the moral law.

But this argument is deeply flawed. In addition to the problem noted after its first step, it depends upon an equivocation and contradicts its own starting-point. The equivocation is that it depends upon thinking of reason in two different ways: the faculty of reason that distinguishes us from all *other* things in nature is something *empirically observable*, that is, we discover empirically that, for example, we build our structures with the use of reason while ants, bees, or beavers build by instinct and robots build by programs, all merely mimicking our rational processes; but the faculty of reason that is supposed to distinguish our real from our merely apparent nature *cannot* be something empirically observed or discovered. And since nothing that we can discover about ourselves empirically can justify any assertion about our non-empirical, 'real' selves, the fact that we are rational in an empirical sense cannot justify the claim that we are really rational beings 'in ourselves.' Second, Kant's conclusion contradicts his starting-point, because his argument starts by drawing the distinction between ourselves as we appear and ourselves as we really are by insisting upon our complete passivity and domination by the laws of nature, but then concludes by ascribing to us activity or spontaneity self-governed by the laws of reason.

The second objection is not serious, for what Kant actually said at the outset of the argument is that we are passive in our experience of external objects, not in *all* of our conditions; his aim was then to show that our *actions* at the phenomenal level are subject to the moral law because, while our phenomenal representations of external objects are the effect of *other* things in themselves upon us, our phenomenal actions are the effects of our *own* real selves, which are fully rational. The problem with the argument is rather the first objection, that is, the charge that Kant has no real basis for his positive assertion that our real selves *are* genuinely rational except for his illegitimate inference from the phenomenal rationality that distinguishes us from other things in nature to the genuine rationality of our real selves. By his own insistence on the distinction between appearances and things in themselves, he should not be able to infer from a feature of appearances to a similar feature of things in themselves, thus he should not be able to infer from phenomenal rationality to noumenal rationality. Indeed, in the *Critique of Pure Reason* Kant had emphatically made this very point by insisting on a distinction between the noumenon in a 'negative' and 'a positive' sense (A 252) or the 'problematic' and 'assertoric' uses of the concept of the noumenon (A 254–5/B 310–11): the first member of each of these pairs is the thought that we *cannot* know anything about the real nature of things by *any* of our faculties, the second is the thought that while we cannot know the real nature of things by means of our sensibility and our understanding as applied to our sensibility, we *can* know the real nature of things by means of our faculty of *reason* alone. But in the first *Critique* Kant *rejected* the possibility that we could know the noumenon in a positive sense. Yet if he were to accept this restriction now, he would not have any information about our noumenal selves at all; as far as he would be entitled to know, our noumenal selves are just as likely to be thoroughly irrational as genuinely rational.[7]

This seems to be an irremediable flaw in Kant's argument that we human beings really are rational agents because we are rational agents at the noumenal level. But there is yet another problem, namely, that even if the argument did work, then it would prove too much: if we were really thoroughly rational beings at the noumenal level, then all of our actions at the phenomenal level would be the product of our fully rational noumenal character, and would necessarily be in full compliance with the demands of morality. In other words, if our noumenal nature were necessarily fully rational, there would be no way to explain our performance of any actions *contrary* to reason, that is, *immoral* actions, or, however such actions were to be explained, they could not be attributed to our real characters and selves. We would be genuinely responsible only for our moral actions, and not responsible for our immoral actions at all, which must come from somewhere else altogether and merely appear to be ours. This would certainly fly in the face of all morality and common sense.

This objection to Kant's argument is inevitable given his decision to try to prove that the moral law is the *causal* law of our real will. And it was quickly raised. Karl Leonhard Reinhold, who originally popularized Kant in the first series of his *Letters on the Kantian Philosophy* (1786–7),[8] clearly formulated it in the second volume of his letters (1792) when he charged precisely that Kant confused the moral law as a rational norm for the actions of the free will with a causal law for those actions themselves :

From the confusion of the to be sure self-active but nothing less than free action of practical reason – which gives nothing but the law – with the action of the will – which acts as a **pure** will only insofar as it freely grasps this law – nothing less than the impossibility of freedom for all **immoral** actions must follow. As soon as it is assumed that the freedom of the **pure will** consists merely in the self-activity of practical reason, then one must also concede that the **impure will**, which is not effected through practical reason, is by no means free.[9]

The great British utilitarian Henry Sidgwick raised what is basically the same problem in a famous article in 1888, writing that if 'Freedom is said to be a "causality according to immutable laws"... it must mean that the will, *qua* free, acts in accordance with these laws; – the human being, doubtless, often acts contrary to them; but then, according to this view, its choice in such actions is determined not "freely" but "mechanically".'[10]

Now Sidgwick thought that Kant had two different conceptions of free will, this conception on which the will is necessarily rational and therefore itself incapable of being the source of immoral actions, and another, 'neutral' conception, on which the will can choose either to be rational or not, thus to perform only moral actions or not. This was the same solution that Reinhold recommended. And indeed in his later works, beginning with the *Critique of Practical Reason* – published in 1788, thus even before Reinhold's criticism – this is the approach that Kant himself would take. Thus, in the second *Critique* he does not attempt to infer that we are subject to the moral law from the premises that we are truly free and that the moral law is the causal law of the free will; rather, he argues that we are immediately conscious of our obligation under the moral law as a 'fact of reason,' and then infers from the premises that we acknowledge this obligation and that we must be *capable* of fulfilling any genuine obligation that we must be free to conform our actions to the moral law, but are not metaphysically necessitated to do so.[11] In *Religion within the Boundaries of Mere Reason*, Kant would reiterate the key premise of this argument, that 'duty commands nothing but what we can do,' so that 'if the moral law commands that we **ought** to be better human beings now, it inescapably follows that we must be **capable** of being better human beings,' numerous times.[12] The latter premise solves the Reinhold–Sidgwick problem precisely because even if 'ought' implies 'can' it does not imply 'does.' But this alternative form of argument undermines Kant's strategy in *Groundwork* III for proving that the moral law is a binding norm for us: if Kant cannot argue that the moral law is the causal law of the free will without making immoral action inexplicable, then he still needs both an independent account of why we are really obligated by the moral law and an independent proof that we are free to live up to it although not metaphysically necessitated to do so.

The *Critique of Practical Reason* shortcuts the first of these tasks by simply asserting that our obligation under the moral law is a fact of reason, and offers an elaborate solution to the second task. Kant does not say in that work that he is withdrawing the approach of the *Groundwork*. And he certainly does not say within the *Groundwork* itself that he is backing off from his metaphysical argument. Nevertheless, in the remaining pages of Section III Kant does subtly shift his ground, treating the moral law as an ideal to which we must aspire, not the causal law of our free will, and appealing to transcendental idealism to establish only that it may be possible for us to fulfill the demands of morality, not that it is impossible for us not to. This may mean, however, that he has nothing more to say about why we must regard the moral law as the ideal for our own behavior, and that we must remain content with the appeal to our sense of dignity which seemed to be his last word on this central issue in Section II.

4. FROM METAPHYSICAL NECESSITY TO MORAL IDEAL

Kant's next step is to claim that the two-level model of human action that he has just introduced solves the problem of the possibility of the categorical imperative by showing how we can be both obligated and able to perform actions contrary to our inclinations: mere inclinations would be the only determinants of our actions if our actions took place entirely at the phenomenal level, but our actions do not take place solely at that level, for they also have a ground at the noumenal in the determination of our will in accordance with pure reason. However, Kant's conception of noumenal reason as a ground for our phenomenal actions now seems to undergo a subtle transformation: he backs off from treating the moral law as the *causal* law of the free will, which is what created the problem that an immoral action could not be a free action at all, and instead treats pure reason as a *possible* ground for our actions, a ground we *can* choose to use but are not *metaphysically* obligated to choose. Kant now separates the role of transcendental idealism as the explanation of the possibility of our acting in accordance with the moral law from its role as the source of the moral law as the ideal to which we should strive to conform our actions, although he as it were continues to hope that it is the latter as well as the former.

That Kant now uses transcendental idealism to explain the possibility but not the necessity of our acting in accordance with the moral law becomes evident as soon as he uses it to answer the question 'How is a categorical imperative possible?', because, as he made clear

KANT'S *GROUNDWORK FOR THE METAPHYSICS OF MORALS*

at the beginning of Section II, the moral law takes the form of a categorical imperative precisely insofar as it is obligatory for beings who do *not* automatically behave in accordance with it. Kant says that if I were 'a mere piece of the world of sense my actions would have to be taken to be entirely in accord with the natural law of desires and inclinations, hence of heteronomy,' and that if I were 'a mere member of the world of understanding all of my actions would be perfectly in accord with the principle of the autonomy of the pure will,' and then continues '**but that since the world of understanding contains the ground of the world of sense and hence of its laws**' I must regard the 'laws of the former, i.e., of reason, which in the idea of freedom contains the law thereof, . . . as an imperative and the actions that are in accord with this principle as duties' (4:453–4). In this complicated chain of thought, Kant does not treat my membership in the intelligible world, that is, the freedom of my will at the noumenal level from the causal determinism of desire and inclination at the phenomenal level, as making it inevitable that I will act as morality requires; rather, he states my membership in the noumenal world to be the ground of my moral obligation to act in accord with the moral law and of the possibility of my so acting. But the description of the moral law even in the face of my membership in both worlds as an *imperative* means that it is something I must struggle to conform to and that my success in this struggle is not guaranteed.

The same conclusion follows from the next paragraph, where Kant says that

> Categorical imperatives are possible through the fact that the idea of freedom makes me into a member of an intelligible world through which, if I were that alone, all of my actions **would** always be in accord with the autonomy of the will, but since I at the same time intuit myself as a member of the world of the senses, they **ought** to accord with that, which **categorical** ought represents a synthetic *a priori* proposition, in that to my will affected by sensible desires the idea of the same will but belonging to the world of understanding, pure and practical for itself, is added, which contains the supreme condition of the former in accordance with reason . . . (4:454)

In this sentence, certainly one of the most complicated in the *Groundwork*, Kant makes two key points. First, he reiterates the claim that if I were a member of either the sensible world or the intelligible world exclusively, then my actions would automatically be determined by either mere inclination or the moral law respectively, but that since I am a member of both worlds then the moral law is a norm to which I ought to conform my behavior and to which it is possible for me to conform my behavior – but my membership in the intelligible world does not guarantee that my actions in the phenomenal world will conform to the moral law. Second, Kant once again uses his concept of the synthetic *a priori* to capture this dual character of human nature: while it might be analytically true that a purely rational being would conform its behavior to the moral law, it is synthetically true that human beings with their dual nature ought to and can conform their behavior to that law. This synthetic proposition is still known *a priori*, however, because we know that we ought to and can observe the moral law not on the basis of experience (4:455, 459) but, supposedly, on the basis of the purely philosophical knowledge of our dual nature itself, as explicated in the central argument of Section III.

Kant also emphasizes that the noumenal basis of our own phenomenal character implies only our obligation under the moral law and the possibility of our living up to this obligation but not the inevitability of our doing so by means of an illustration. He says that even the 'most hardened villain' wishes to be honest, sympathetic, and benevolent when examples of such virtues are placed before him, 'but he cannot bring it about on account of his inclinations and impulses, although he at the same time wishes to be free of such burdensome inclinations.' His wish to be virtuous proves that he 'transports himself in his thoughts into an entirely different order of things,' but the fact that he cannot free himself from his burdensome inclinations proves that his transport into this other order of things does not automatically determine his actual behavior. Kant concludes his discussion of this example by saying that 'The moral ought is thus his own necessary volition as a member of an intelligible world and is thought of by him as an ought only insofar as he at the same time considers himself as a member of the sensible world' (4:454–5): this means that as a being with one foot in the intelligible world, even the hardened criminal necessarily recognizes or 'wills' the normative force of the moral law, but not that he necessarily acts in accordance with it. If the latter were true, then he would not have to think of the moral law as an 'ought,' that is, an imperative.

In suggesting that our dual nature proves the possibility of our acting in accordance with the moral law but not the necessity of our doing so, Kant in fact reverts to the interpretation of transcendental idealism that he had adopted in the *Critique of Pure Reason* and that he would maintain in later works such as the *Critique of Practical Reason* and *Religion within the Boundaries of Mere Reason*. This becomes clear as he proceeds to resolve the 'dialectic of reason' to which he now turns. The dialectic arises from the threat that 'freedom is only an **idea** of reason, the objective reality of which is doubtful' and cannot be proven from any experience, while 'nature,' thus determinism, 'is a **concept of the understanding** which proves its reality from examples of experience and necessarily must so prove it' (4:455). The danger of this dialectic, of course, is that if the reality of determinism is certain but that of freedom is doubtful, then we will think (like the hardened criminal) that we cannot live up to the moral law no matter how much we claim we wish to, and then use that as an excuse not even to try. In order to avoid this dialectic, Kant states, we must be able to 'presuppose that there is no true contradiction between freedom and the natural necessity of the very same human actions' (4:456). To show that there is no such contradiction, however, we must simply appeal to the distinction between appearances and things in themselves. 'For that a **thing in appearance** (belonging to the sensible world) is subject to certain laws from which the very same thing **as thing** or being **in itself** is independent contains not the least contradiction,' and the fact that the human being 'must think of and represent himself in this twofold way rests, as far as the first way is concerned, on the consciousness of himself as an object affected through the senses, and as far as the second is concerned, on the consciousness of himself as intelligence, i.e., as independent in the use of his reason from sensible impressions (hence as belonging to the world of understanding)' (4:457). But that there is no contradiction in the idea that a single being might determine its choice of actions by the moral law of pure reason rather than by mere inclinations does not, of course, guarantee that it will do the former rather than the latter. The twofold conception of human nature is sufficient to refute the 'fatalist' who would undermine all moral philosophy by means of the assertion that a person with criminal inclinations *cannot possibly* overcome them (4:456), but it does not prove that anyone *necessarily will* choose to act as a purely rational and hence moral being.

Indeed, as Kant continues the argument of the *Groundwork* he seems to weaken the initial argument of Section III even further. The initial argument used transcendental idealism to prove that the moral law is the causal law of the noumenal will, which is in turn the ground of all our phenomenal actions. Now Kant claims that although reason does not 'overstep its boundaries' when it merely '**thinks** itself into a world of understanding' as it would if it tried to '**intuit or sense** itself' into such a world (4:458), at the same time 'reason would overstep all its boundaries if it undertook to **explain how** pure reason can be practical, which would be entirely the same as explaining **how freedom is possible**' (4:458–9). Rather, he continues, 'freedom is a mere idea,' not demonstrated by any experience, but 'valid only as a necessary presupposition of reason in a being that believes itself to be conscious of a will, i.e., of a faculty different from a mere faculty of desire (namely of determining itself to act as an intelligence, hence in accordance with laws of reason, independent from natural instincts)' (4:459). Now freedom becomes an idea or presupposition that can be *defended* by transcendental idealism, for even the mere possibility that transcendental idealism is true means that no one can prove that the determinism that we take to hold in the empirically observable world of nature is the whole story about human conduct, but not something that can actually be *proved* by a proof of the truth of transcendental idealism itself.

So after what appeared to be a step over the brink into metaphysics and then a step back from the brink, where are we left? Kant's attempt to prove both that the moral law is our binding obligation and that we are capable of living up to it by proving directly that our 'authentic selves' simply do act in accordance with the moral law has foundered. In general terms, the argument depended upon using a positive rather than negative sense of the noumenal; specifically, it depended on inferring that the reason that distinguishes us from other things within the phenomenal world is also what distinguishes us from the phenomenal world altogether, and Kant had no justification for that. And if he had succeeded in proving that the moral law of pure reason is also the causal law of our will at its deepest level, he would have proved too much, for he would have made the free but immoral action impossible, and this would both contradict common-sense morality as well as his own conception of the moral law as a categorical imperative, that is, something that we can freely chose to obey, although often with a struggle, but that we can also freely choose to disobey. If we have to choose between the idea that the moral law is the causal law of the noumenal will and the concept of the categorical imperative as an accurate reflection of both the appeal and difficulty of morality in the human condition, the latter seems a much better choice.

And what about transcendental idealism itself, even if it would not imply everything that Kant apparently hoped it would at the outset of Section III – has Kant proved that doctrine in the *Groundwork*? It cannot be said that he has: in lieu of the complex arguments for this doctrine that he offered in the *Critique of Pure Reason*, in the *Groundwork* he offered only the single argument that the causal character of our perception of external objects proves that there is a fundamental difference between the representation of those objects and the real character of those objects themselves, and this argument, as we saw, is problematic. The best that can be said is that Kant must really be relying on his theoretical philosophy for the proof of transcendental idealism, and that this can prove no more than that it cannot be proven to be impossible that we can be moved by pure reason and the demands of morality alone, even in radical conflict with our sensory desires and inclinations.

But this may be enough for at least some of Kant's purposes in the *Groundwork*. Indeed, in one of his closing moves he cleverly exploits our necessary ignorance rather than knowledge of the real nature of our will to defend a feature of our moral life that might otherwise seem difficult to reconcile with his principles. In spite of his insistence that the fundamental *principle* of morality cannot be derived from any feelings, Kant is also convinced that some form of 'moral feeling' is an ineliminable component of human moral conduct – that the decision to act as pure practical reason dictates does not determine our action in spite of *all* the feelings that we might have, but rather that it works precisely by producing a powerful moral feeling that can determine our actions, at the phenomenal, natural level, instead of other feelings that might not reliably lead to moral actions or that would reliably lead to immoral actions.[13] Kant thinks it is a mystery that the intellectual activity of pure reason should produce a feeling in the phenomenal world, but also thinks that this mystery cannot be an objection to his model of moral conduct precisely because the relation between the noumenal and the phenomenal is in general a mystery:

The subjective impossibility of **explaining** the freedom of the will is identical with the impossibility of discovering and making comprehensible the **interest** which the human being can take in moral laws; and yet he really does take an interest in them, the foundation of which in us we call the moral feeling, which is falsely taken by some as the standard for our moral judging, where it must rather be regarded as the **subjective** effect that the law has on the will, for which reason alone provides the objective ground. (4:459–60).

Here Kant takes one last swipe at the 'moral sense' theorists who would make our mere feelings of approbation and disapprobation into the principle of morality, but at the same time suggests his own view that moral feeling is the effect of the will's choice to adhere to the moral law and in turn the cause of our particular moral actions in the phenomenal world. The mere possibility that our will can be determined by pure practical reason is enough to make this model of action possible, and presumably Kant thinks it is beyond that made plausible because it fits with what he takes to be a plausible moral phenomenology on the one hand and the conviction that the ultimate source of morality is reason rather than inclination on the other.

Second, the mere possibility that we can live up to the ideal of morality may be all we really need to make our efforts to live up to it rational if that ideal is sufficiently compelling in its own right. Kant seems to flirt one last time with a stronger interpretation of the implications of transcendental idealism. He starts by saying, just as the last paragraph suggested, that an 'explanation of how and why the **universality of a maxim as a law** interests us is entirely impossible for us human beings.' But then he seems to fall back into a more positive use of his metaphysics:

Only this much is certain: that it does not have validity for us **because it interests us** (for that is heteronomy and the dependence of practical reason on sensibility, namely on a feeling lying at its basis, in which case it can never be morally legislative), rather that it interests us because it is valid for us as human beings, since it has its origin from our will as intelligence, hence from our authentic self: **but what belongs to mere appearance is necessarily subordinated to the constitution of the thing in itself by reason.** (4:460–1).

Kant's claim that intelligence, that is, pure practical reason, is our authentic self, is a metaphysical claim, and he once again seems to be hoping that he does not need to prove that pure practical reason is our ultimate *norm* because at the deepest level it is simply a *fact* that we are in accordance with it. And his bold-face statement that what belongs to mere appearance, that is, inclinations, is necessarily subordinated to what we are in ourselves, namely purely rational wills, again raises the danger that it will be impossible to allow for free yet immoral actions. But Kant finally draws back from this metaphysical precipice:

> But now **how** pure reason, without other incentives taken from who knows where can be practical of itself, i.e., how the mere **principle of the universal validity of all of its maxims as laws** . . . can by itself provide an incentive and an interest that would be called purely **moral**, or in other words: **how pure reason can be practical** – to explain that is entirely beyond the capacity of all human reason, and all effort and labor in seeking an explanation of it is wasted . . . .the idea of a pure world of understanding, as a whole of all intelligences, to which we ourselves as rational beings (although on the other side at the same time members of the world of the senses) belong, always remains a usable and permissible idea for the sake of a rational belief, even though all knowledge has an end at its boundary, in order to effect in us a lively interest in the moral law through the magnificent ideal of a universal realm of **ends in themselves** (rational beings) to which we can belong as members only if we carefully conduct ourselves in accordance with maxims of freedom as if they were laws of nature. (4:461–3).

Here Kant claims that the image of a realm of ends that can only be realized through carefully maintaining the universalizability of our maxims or treating them as if they were to be laws of nature is a 'magnificent ideal,' and all we really need to know is that because of the ultimate limits of human knowledge it could never be proven that we are incapable of living up to this ideal.

Thus, in the end, Kant admits that he does not have to prove that we necessarily act in accordance with the moral law, or even prove in some positive way that it is always possible for us to act in accordance with it; all he has to show, which he takes himself to have done, is that because of the ultimate limits of human knowledge, even knowledge about the inmost workings of our own wills, nobody can prove that it is impossible for us to live up to the magnificent ideal of morality.

But then this brings us back to our outstanding question about Section II of the *Groundwork*, namely, can we prove that the goal of a realm of ends in which each is treated as an end and never as a means because each acts only on universalizable maxims is the sole thing of unconditional value? In the end, Section III has nothing to add to what Section II already had to say on that issue, namely, that we simply recognize an incomparable dignity in acting in accord with our own reason rather than being pushed around by mere impulses and inclinations. If that ideal seems deeply moving to you, then Kant has shown how a formal principle of morality and a complete system of duties can be founded upon it. If that ideal does not seem moving to you, then he has nothing more to say to you. He can tell you that if you base your morality upon what you take to be the commands of God or the natural desire of either yourself or all human beings for happiness or on any other inclination, then you are allowing your will to be determined heteronomously rather than determining it autonomously – but that will not move you unless you are already committed to the supreme importance of autonomy. Kant's moral philosophy is a brilliant account of what it takes to achieve autonomy, but in the last analysis its force must rest on the intrinsic appeal of autonomy as an ideal for human life.

Study Questions

1. In what sense are a free will and a will under moral laws the same?
2. Can transcendental idealism prove that we are capable of living up to the moral law?
3. Can transcendental idealism prove that we ought to live up to the moral law?
4. If transcendental idealism cannot prove this, is there anything that can?

NOTES

1. CONTEXT

1 For details on this stage of Kant's education, see Heiner F. Klemme, editor, *Die Schule Immanuel Kants: Mit dem Text von Christian Schiffert über das Königsberger Collegium Fredericianum*, Kant-Forschungen Band 6 (Hamburg: Felix Meiner, 1994).
2 For a good account of Kant's university years, see Manfred Kuehn, *Kant: A Biography* (Cambridge: Cambridge University Press, 2001), Chapter 2.
3 See Kuehn, *Kant*, pp. 86–95.
4 The story of Kant's appointment to this chair does not reflect entirely well on him: he got the chair by proposing to the king that its current occupant be moved over to the vacant chair in mathematics without telling his colleague about his plan. See Kuehn, *Kant*, pp. 188–9.
5 See Anthony Ashley Cooper, Third Earl of Shaftesbury, *Charackteristicks of Men, Manner, Opinions, Times*, edited by Philip Ayres, two volumes (Oxford: Clarendon Press, 1999), specifically *Sensus Communis: An Essay on the Freedom of Wit and Humour*, Part II, Section III, at vol. I, pp. 55–7.

2. OVERVIEW OF THEMES

1 I translate this passage from the Johann Friedrich Kaehler transcription from the summer semester of 1777, published in Immanuel Kant, *Vorlesung zur Moralphilosophie*, edited by Werner Stark, with an introduction by Manfred Kuehn (Berlin and New York: Walter de Gruyter & Co., 2004), pp. 176–7, 178, 180. A similar version of the passage is still found in the transcription by Georg Ludwig Collins from the winter semester of 1784–5, which can be found in Immanuel Kant, *Lectures on Ethics*, edited by Peter Heath and J.B. Schneewind, translated by Peter Heath (Cambridge: Cambridge University Press, 1997), pp. 125–8.
2 Kant, *Vorlesung zur Moralphilosophie*, pp. 179–80.
3 Reflection 6598 (19:103), translated in Immanuel Kant, *Notes and Fragments*, edited by Paul Guyer, translated by Curtis Bowman, Paul

Guyer, and Frederick Rauscher (Cambridge: Cambridge University Press, 2005), p. 420.

4 Reflection 5444 (18:183), in *Notes and Fragments*, p. 414.

5 Reflection 6856 (19:181), in *Notes and Fragments*, p. 441.

6 Kant, *Naturrecht Feyerabend*, 27:1321–2.

7 Reflection 6596 (19:101), in *Notes and Fragments*, p. 420.

8 Reflection 6864 (19:184), in *Notes and Fragments*, p. 443.

9 Reflection 6850 (19:178), in *Notes and Fragments*, p. 439.

10 Reflection 6621 (19:114–15), in *Notes and Fragments*, pp. 425–6.

11 Reflection 6820 (19:172), in *Notes and Fragments*, pp. 437–8.

12 Reflection 6851 (19:179), in *Notes and Fragments*, p. 439.

13 Kant, *Naturrecht Feyerabend*, 27:1321.

14 *Loc. cit.*

15 Kant, *Naturrecht Feyerabend*, 27:1319.

16 Reflection 6862 (19:183), in *Notes and Fragments*, p. 443.

17 See Kant, *Anthropology from a Pragmatic Point of View*, translated by Mary J. Gregor (The Hague: Martinus Nijhoff, 1972), §82 (7:268–9), pp. 135–6.

18 Kant, *Inquiry concerning the Distinctness of the Principles of Natural Theology and Morality*, Reflection 4, §2, 2:299; in Kant, *Theoretical Philosophy 1755–1770*, edited by David E. Walford with the collaboration of Ralf Meerbote (Cambridge: Cambridge University Press, 1992), p. 273.

19 Reflection 6713 (19:138), in *Notes and Fragments*, p. 430.

20 Reflection 6975 (19:218), in *Notes and Fragments*, p. 454.

21 Reflection 7248 (19:294), in *Notes and Fragments*, p. 474.

22 Reflection 6867 (19:186), in *Notes and Fragments*, p. 444.

23 See Reflection 7202 (19:278), in *Notes and Fragments*, p. 466.

24 Reflection 7202 (19:277), in *Notes and Fragments*, p. 465.

3. READING THE TEXT: PREFACE

1 See David Hume, *A Treatise of Human Nature*, Book I, Part III, sections 6–9, and *An Enquiry concerning Human Understanding*, Section 4, Part 2.

2 See also *Immanuel Kant's Logic: A Manual for Lectures*, edited by Gottlob Benjamin Jäsche, §1, in Kant, *Lectures on Logic*, edited by J. Michael Young (Cambridge: Cambridge University Press, 1992), p. 589.

3 *Critique of Pure Reason*, A 305–33/B 362–90.

4 See *PracR*, 5:30, and *Religion*, 6:45, 47, 49n., 50, 62, and 67.

5 *Prolegomena to Any Future Metaphysics*, §4, 4:274–5.

4. READING THE TEXT: SECTION I. FROM THE GOOD WILL TO THE FORMULA OF UNIVERSAL LAW

1 Kant frequently refers to the case of Cato, which he could have known about from Addison's play, which was translated into German, from Johann Christoph Gottsched's play *Der sterbende Cato* (1724), which

pirated chunks of Addison's play, or from his own reading in Roman history. A modern edition of Addison's play is *Cato: A Tragedy, and Selected Essays*, edited by Christine Dunn Henderson and Mark E. Yellin (Indianapolis: Liberty Fund, 2004). As far as I know, Kant never refers to Goethe's *Werther*.

2 He later does so in the *Metaphysics of Morals*, Doctrine of Virtue, Introduction, Section V.B, 6:388.
3 See *Metaphysics of Morals*, Doctrine of Virtue, Introduction, Section IV, 6:386.
4 *Religion*, 6:21; in Wood and di Giovanni, p. 70.
5 See *Religion*, 6:35; Wood and di Giovanni, pp. 81–2.
6 *Religion*, 6:44; Wood and di Giovanni, p. 89.
7 *Religion*, 6:36; Wood and di Giovanni, p. 83.
8 Translation by A.B. Bullock, cited by H.J. Paton, *The Categorical Imperative: A Study in Kant's Moral Philosophy* (London: Hutchinson, 1947), p. 48, who in turn took it from Hastings Rashdall, *The Theory of Good and Evil* (London, 1907), vol. I, p. 120. It came originally from the collection *Xenien* by Schiller and Goethe.
9 See Michael Stocker, 'The Schizophrenia of Modern Ethical Theory,' *Journal of Philosophy* 73 (1976): 453–66, and Bernard Williams, 'Persons, Character, and Morality,' in his *Moral Luck: Philosophical Papers, 1973–1980* (Cambridge: Cambridge University Press, 1981), p. 17.
10 Originally published in *The Philosophical Review* 90 (1981): 359–82, reprinted in her book *The Practice of Moral Judgment* (Cambridge, MA: Harvard University Press, 1993), pp. 1–22.
11 Henson's article is 'What Kant Might Have Said: Moral Worth and the Over-determination of Dutiful Action,' *The Philosophical Review* 88 (1979): 39–54. Herman's discussion begins on p. 7 of *The Practice of Moral Judgment*.
12 Herman, *The Practice of Moral Judgment*, p. 13.
13 Herman, *The Practice of Moral Judgment*, p. 15.
14 *Kant on the Metaphysics of Morals* (*Vigilantius*), 26:671; in *Lectures on Ethics*, edited by Heath and Schneewind, p. 404.
15 Herman, *The Practice of Moral Judgment*, pp. 4–5.
16 Kant's clearest account of the theory of the complete good may be in Section I of the 1793 essay 'On the common saying: That may be correct in theory but it is of no use in practice.'

5. READING THE TEXT: SECTION II. FORMULATING THE CATEGORICAL IMPERATIVE

1 See notably H.J. Paton, *The Categorical Imperative: A Study in Kant's Moral Philosophy* (London: Hutchinson, 1947), pp. 146–64.
2 This analysis of a maxim has been suggested by a number of writers beginning with Onora Nell (O'Neill), *Acting on Principle: An Essay on Kantian Ethics* (New York: Columbia University Press, 1975), pp. 34–42.

3 This is an example that Kant considers in a notorious essay of 1797 'On a supposed right to lie from philanthropy' (translated in Gregor, *Practical Philosophy*, pp. 605–15). He argues there that lying even to save an innocent life is prohibited; although his argument may be unconvincing, however, it does not turn on the simple fallacy of inferring that because lying is prohibited in some circumstances it is prohibited in all circumstances.

4 For the idea of a 'practical contradiction,' see Christine M. Korsgaard, 'Kant's Formula of Universal Law,' in her *Creating the Kingdom of Ends* (Cambridge, MA: Harvard University Press, 1996), pp. 77–105.

5 For this interpretation of the relation between the first two formulations of the categorical imperative, see especially Onora O'Neill, 'Universal laws and ends-in themselves,' *Monist* 72 (1989): 341–62, reprinted in her *Constructions of Reason: Explorations of Kant's Practical Philosophy* (Cambridge: Cambridge University Press, 1989), pp. 126–44.

6 Jean-Jacques Rousseau, *The Social Contract*, Book II, chapter 6; translation from Nicholas Dent, *Rousseau* (London and New York: Routledge, 2005), p. 134.

7 In order to prevent confusion when reading Kant's other writings in moral philosophy, it should be mentioned that Kant does not always use the term 'interest' in the perjorative sense assumed in the passage we have just discussed. In the *Critique of Practical Reason*, he speaks in entirely positive terms of reason's 'interest' in the moral law and in resolving any contradictions or 'antinomies' that might threaten our recognition of its unconditional authority; see especially 5:19–20, where Kant says that 'To every faculty of the mind' including reason 'one can attribute an **interest**, that is, a principle that contains the condition under which alone its exercise is promoted,' and that reason 'determines the interest of all the powers of the mind but itself determines its own' (Gregor, p. 236).

8 See especially Allen W. Wood, 'The Supreme Principle of Morality,' in Paul Guyer, editor, *The Cambridge Companion to Kant and Modern Philosophy* (Cambridge: Cambridge University Press, 2006), pp. 342–80, especially 358–60.

9 Arthur O. Lovejoy listed no fewer than eighteen senses of 'nature' just within aesthetics; see his '"Nature" as Aesthetic Norm,' originally *Modern Language Notes* (1927): 444–50, reprinted in his *Essays in the History of Ideas* (New York: Capricorn Books, 1960), pp. 69–77.

10 Korsgaard, 'Kant's Formula of Humanity,' in her *Creating the Kingdom of Ends*, pp. 106–32, at pp. 122–3. For endorsement of a similar argument, see Allen W. Wood, *Kant's Ethical Thought* (Cambridge: Cambridge University Press, 1999), pp. 130–2.

11 Kant, *Vorlesung zur Moralphilosophie*, p. 216; cf. Immanuel Kant, *Lectures on Ethics*, edited by Peter Heath and J.B. Schneewind, translated by Peter Heath (Cambridge: Cambridge University Press, 1997), p. 144.

12 *Vorlesung zur Moralphilosophie*, p. 218; *Lectures on Ethics*, p. 145.

13 *Vorlesgung zur Moralphilosophie*, p. 173; *Lectures on Ethics*, p. 123.

14 See Georg Wilhelm Friedrich Hegel, *Natural Law: The Scientific Ways of Treating Natural Law, Its Place in Moral Philosophy, and Its Relation to the Positive Sciences of Law* (1802–3), translated by T.M. Knox (Philadelphia: University of Pennsylvania Press, 1975), pp. 76–8. Hegel takes up the form of the example that Kant uses in the *Critique of Practical Reason*, where the promise is one to return a deposit, and charges that Kant's example 'posits' the institution of property and property-rights. See also Hegel, *Elements of the Philosophy of Right* (1820), edited by Allen W. Wood, translated by H.B. Nisbet (Cambridge: Cambridge University Press, 1991), §135, pp. 162–3.

15 See Bruce Aune, *Kant's Theory of Morals* (Princeton: Princeton University Press, 1979), Chapter 1, pp. 28–34, Chapter 3, pp. 86–90.

16 For example, Nicholas Rescher, *Kant and the Reach of Reason: Studies in Kant's Theory of Rational Systematization* (Cambridge: Cambridge University Press, 2000), chapter 8, pp. 200–29.

17 These examples come from Barbara Herman, *The Practice of Moral Judgment*, pp. 138–9, and Onora Nell (O'Neill), *Acting on Principle: An Essay on Kantian Ethics*, p. 76.

18 Barbara Herman, 'Mutual Aid and Respect for Persons,' in *The Practice of Moral Judgment*, pp. 45–72.

19 See Allen W. Wood, 'Humanity as an End in Itself,' in Paul Guyer, editor, *Kant's Groundwork of the Metaphysics of Morals: Critical Essays* (Lanham: Rowman & Littlefield, 1998), pp. 165–88, or Wood, *Kant's Ethical Thought*, pp. 139–41.

20 Unfortunately, Kant seems to lapse into a merely prudential argument three sections later, when he writes 'Everyone who finds himself in need wishes to be helped by others. But if he lets his maxim of being unwilling to assist others in turn when they are in need become public . . . then everyone would likewise deny him assistance when he himself is in need' (*MM*, 'Doctrine of Virtue,' §30, 6:453). Here he makes it sound as if the problem is that if one's policy of indifference to others becomes known then it will *cause* others to become indifferent to oneself, so that such a policy would be imprudent in circumstances where it is likely to become known (which is highly likely). Kant should have stuck with the argument of §27, which is clearly not a merely prudential argument.

21 See Samuel Pufendorf, *The Whole Duty of Man, According to the Law of Nature*, translated by Andrew Tooke, edited by Ian Hunter and David Saunders (Indianapolis: Liberty Fund, 2003), Book I, Chapter 2, Section XIV, p. 50.

22 See for example a version of the textbook that Kant used in his lectures on natural right, Gottfried Achenwall and Johann Stephan Pütter, *Elementa Iuris Naturae/Anfangsgründe des Naturrechts*, edited by Jan Schröder (Frankfurt am Main: Insel Verlag, 1995), Introduction, Chapter 4, §177.

23 On issues discussed in this paragraph, see also Onora O'Neill, 'Instituting Principles: Between Duty and Action,' in Mark Timmons, editor, *Kant's Metaphysics of Morals: Interpretative Essays* (Oxford: Oxford University Press, 2002), pp. 331–47.

NOTES

24 For more detailed discussion of the duties of virtue, see Mary J. Gregor, *Laws of Freedom: A Study of Kant's Method of Applying the Categorical Imperative in the* Metaphysik der Sitten (Oxford: Basil Blackwell, 1963), chapters VIII–XII; Allen Wood, 'Humanity as an End in Itself' and *Kant's Ethical Thought*, chapter 4.

25 For this terminology, see Wood, *Kant's Ethical Thought*, pp. 102–7.

26 This example is from Onora Nell (O'Neill), *Acting on Principle*, pp. 71–2, who borrows the name 'Ignatz MacGillycuddy' from an example in Marcus G. Singer, *Generalization in Ethics: An Essay in the Logic of Ethics, with the Rudiments of a System of Moral Philosophy*, new edition (New York: Athenaeum, 1971), pp. 87–8. Both of these works contain important discussions of the issue of the application of the categorical imperative.

27 For this response, see Herman, 'Moral Deliberation and the Derivation of Duties,' in *The Practice of Moral Judgment*, pp. 138–9.

28 Wood, *Kant's Ethical Thought*, p. 100.

6. READING THE TEXT: SECTION III. THE CATEGORICAL IMPERATIVE APPLIES TO US

1 Thus, Kant's negative and positive definitions of freedom must be sharply distinguished from the 'Two Concepts of Liberty' famously distinguished by Isaiah Berlin in the paper of that name in his inaugural lecture at Oxford University in 1958 and reprinted in his *Four Essays on Liberty* (Oxford: Oxford University Press, 1969), pp. 118–72. For Berlin, the 'negative' and 'positive' senses of liberty are two *alternative* political ideals, one the ideal of leaving the individual as much freedom from interference by government as possible (the ideal of the classical liberalism of Locke and Mill), the other an ideal of human self-realization that can only be achieved through government (the ideal of political idealism as in Hegel and his successors and of twentieth-century liberalism as some understand it). Kant's contrast is not political, and is rather one between an incomplete characterization of freedom in general and a characterization that completes the former by revealing its only possible basis.

2 See *Critique of Pure Reason*, 'The Antinomy of Pure Reason,' 'Third Conflict,' e.g., A 446/B 474.

3 See *Critique of Pure Reason*, 'Canon of Pure Reason,' especially A 806–16/B 834–44; *Critique of Practical Reason*, 'Dialectic of Pure Practical Reason,' especially 5:107–19; and 'On the common saying: That may be correct in theory, but it is of no use in practice,' Part 1, 8:278–89.

4 In the 'Transcendental Aesthetic' of the *Critique of Pure Reason*, as revised in its second edition, Kant offers four different arguments for the distinction between appearances and things in themselves (A 42–9/B 59–72). For discussion of the complexities of Kant's arguments for transcendental idealism, see among other works Paul Guyer, *Kant and the Claims of Knowledge* (Cambridge: Cambridge University Press, 1987),

Part V; Rae Langton, *Kantian Humility* (Oxford: Oxford University Press, 1998); and Henry E. Allison, *Kant's Transcendental Idealism: an Interpretation and Defense*, revised edition (New Haven: Yale University Press, 2004), Parts 1–2.

5 See David Hume, *A Treatise of Human Nature* (1739–40), Book I, Part III, sections II–VI, and *An Enquiry concerning Human Understanding* (1748), Sections 4–5, 7.

6 Kant first made this clear in the 1764 essay 'An Attempt to Introduce the Concept of Negative Magnitudes into Philosophy,' Section 3, 2:189–97.

7 Precisely as Arthur Schopenhauer was to assert, on what he took to be Kantian principles, a generation later; see *The World as Will and Representation* (1819), Book 2.

8 Karl Leonhard Reinhold, *Letters on the Kantian Philosophy*, edited by Karl Ameriks, translated by James Hebbeler (Cambridge: Cambridge University Press, 2005).

9 Karl Leonhard Reinhold, *Briefe über die Kantische Philosophie*, Band 2 (Leipzig, 1792), Brief 8; translated from Rüdiger Bittner and Konrad Cramer, eds., *Materialen zu Kants 'Kritik der praktischen Vernunft'* (Frankfurt am Main: Suhrkamp Verlag, 1975), p. 255. For further discussion of Reinhold's objection, see Henry E. Allison, *Kant's Theory of Freedom* (Cambridge: Cambridge University Press, 1990), pp. 133–5.

10 Henry Sidgwick, 'The Kantian Conception of Free Will,' *Mind* 13 (1888), reprinted in his *Methods of Ethics*, seventh edition (London: Macmillan, 1907), pp. 511–16; quotation from p. 515.

11 See *Critique of Practical Reason*, 5:31–3.

12 These two quotations are from *Religion within the Boundaries of Mere Reason*, 6:47 and 50; see also 6:45, 49n., 62, and 66.

13 Kant will emphasize the existence of such a moral feeling in his discussion of the *feeling* of respect as the incentive of pure practical reason in the *Critique of Practical Reason*, 'Analytic,' chapter III, 5:71–89, and especially in the 'Doctrine of Virtue' of the *Metaphysics of Morals*, Introduction, Section 12, 6:399–403.

SUGGESTIONS FOR FURTHER READING

The literature on Kant's entire philosophy, his moral philosophy in general, and on the *Groundwork* in particular is vast, and much of it is very valuable. Here there is room to list only some of the most important books and collections of articles available in English or English translations.

1. KANT'S LIFE AND GENERAL PHILOSOPHY

Ameriks, Karl. *Interpreting Kant's Critiques.* Oxford: Clarendon Press, 2003.
Guyer, Paul. *Kant.* London: Routledge, 2006.
—— ed. *The Cambridge Companion to Kant.* Cambridge: Cambridge University Press, 1992.
—— ed., *The Cambridge Companion to Kant and Modern Philosophy.* Cambridge: Cambridge University Press, 2006.
Höffe, Otfried. *Immanuel Kant.* Translated by Marshall Farrier. Albany: State University of New York Press, 1994.
Kemp, John. *The Philosophy of Kant.* Oxford: Oxford University Press, 1968.
Kuehn, Manfred. *Kant: A Biography.* Cambridge: Cambridge University Press, 2001.
Wood, Allen W. *Kant.* Oxford: Blackwell Publishing, 2006.

2. THE BACKGROUND AND DEVELOPMENT OF KANT'S MORAL PHILOSOPHY

Beck, Lewis White. *Early German Philosophy: Kant and his Predecessors.* Cambridge, MA: Harvard University Press, 1969.
Broad, C. D. *Five Types of Ethical Theory.* London: Routledge & Kegan Paul, 1930.
Rawls, John. *Lectures on the History of Moral Philosophy.* Edited by Barbara Herman. Cambridge, MA: Harvard University Press, 2000.
Schilpp, Paul Arthur. *Kant's Pre-Critical Ethics.* Evanston: Northwestern University Press, 1938.
Schneewind, J.B. *The Invention of Autonomy: A History of Modern Moral Philosophy.* (Cambridge: Cambridge University Press, 1998), and the

companion anthology of selections from many of the writers he discusses: Schneewind, J.B., ed. *Moral Philosophy from Montaigne to Kant.* Cambridge: Cambridge University Press, 1990.

Ward, Keith. *The Development of Kant's View of Ethics.* Oxford: Basil Blackwell, 1972.

3. TRANSLATIONS OF THE *GROUNDWORK*

Foundations of the Metaphysics of Morals and What is Enlightenment? Translated by Lewis White Beck. Indianapolis and New York: Bobbs-Merrill, 1959.

Groundwork for the Metaphysics of Morals. Translated by Thomas K. Abbott, edited by Lara Denis. Peterborough: Broadview Editions, 2005. With additional selections from Kant and subsequent authors.

Groundwork for the Metaphysics of Morals. Translated by Allen W. Wood. New Haven: Yale University Press, 2002. With essays by J.B. Schneewind, Marcia Baron, Shelly Kagan, and Allen W. Wood.

Groundwork for the Metaphysics of Morals. Translated by Arnulf Zweig, edited by Thomas E. Hill, Jr. and Arnulf Zweig. Oxford: Oxford University Press, 2002. With commentary.

Groundwork of the Metaphysics of Morals. Translated and analyzed by H.J. Paton. New York: Harper & Row, 1964. Originally published under the title *The Moral Law*, London: Hutchinson University Library, 1948.

Groundwork of the Metaphysics of Morals. Edited by Lawrence Pasternack. London: Routledge, 2002. The Paton translation with essays by Thomas E. Hill, Jr., Christine Korsgaard, Onora O'Neill, Henry Allison, Andrews Reath, and Hud Hudson.

4. COMMENTARIES ON THE *GROUNDWORK*

Aune, Bruce. *Kant's Theory of Morals.* Princeton: Princeton University Press, 1979.

Paton, H.J. *The Categorical Imperative: A Study in Kant's Moral Philosophy.* London: Hutchinson, 1947.

Ross, David. *Kant's Ethical Theory: A Commentary on the* Grundlegung zur Metaphysik der Sitten. Oxford: Clarendon Press, 1954.

Sullivan, Roger J. *An Introduction to Kant's Ethics.* Cambridge: Cambridge University Press, 1994.

Wolff, Robert Paul. *The Autonomy of Reason: A Commentary on Kant's Groundwork of the Metaphysics of Morals.* New York: Harper & Row, 1973.

5. OTHER MONOGRAPHS AND SINGLE-AUTHOR COLLECTIONS OF PAPERS ON KANT'S MORAL PHILOSOPHY

Allison, Henry E. *Kant's Theory of Freedom.* Cambridge: Cambridge University Press, 1990.

Baron, Marcia. *Kantian Ethics Almost Without Apology.* Ithaca: Cornell University Press, 1995.

Beck, Lewis White. *A Commentary on Kant's Critique of Practical Reason.* Chicago: University of Chicago Press, 1960.

—— *Studies in the Philosophy of Kant.* Indianapolis: Bobbs-Merrill, 1965.

Cummiskey, David. *Kantian Consequentialism.* New York: Oxford University Press, 1996.

Dean, Richard. *The Value of Humanity in Kant's Moral Theory.* Oxford: Clarendon Press, 2006.

Frierson, Patrick R. *Freedom and Anthropology in Kant's Moral Philosophy.* Cambridge: Cambridge University Press, 2003.

Gregor, Mary J. *The Laws of Freedom: A Study of Kant's Method of Applying the Categorical Imperative in the* Metaphysik der Sitten. Oxford: Basil Blackwell, 1963.

Grenberg, Jeanine. *Kant and the Ethics of Humility: A Story of Dependence, Corruption, and Virtue.* Cambridge: Cambridge University Press, 2005.

Guevara, Daniel. *Kant's Theory of Moral Motivation.* Boulder: Westview Press, 2000.

Guyer, Paul. *Kant on Freedom, Law, and Happiness.* Cambridge: Cambridge University Press, 2000.

—— *Kant's System of Nature and Freedom.* Oxford: Clarendon Press, 2005.

Henrich, Dieter. *The Unity of Reason: Essays on Kant's Philosophy.* Edited by Richard Velkley. Cambridge, MA: Harvard University Press, 1994.

Herman, Barbara. *The Practice of Moral Judgment.* Cambridge, MA: Harvard University Press, 1993.

Hill, Thomas E., Jr. *Dignity and Practical Reason in Kant's Moral Theory.* Ithaca: Cornell University Press, 1992.

—— *Respect, Pluralism, and Justice: Kantian Perspectives.* Oxford: Oxford University Press, 2000.

—— *Human Welfare and Moral Worth: Kantian Perspectives.* Oxford: Oxford University Press, 2002.

Kerstein, Samuel J. *Kant's Search for the Supreme Principle of Morality.* Cambridge: Cambridge University Press, 2002.

Korsgaard, Christine M. *Creating the Kingdom of Ends.* Cambridge: Cambridge University Press, 1996.

—— *The Sources of Normativity.* Edited by Onora O'Neill. Cambridge: Cambridge University Press, 1996.

Louden, Robert B. *Kant's Impure Ethics: From Rational Beings to Human Beings.* New York: Oxford University Press, 2000.

Moore, A.W. *Noble in Reason, Infinite in Faculty: Themes and Variations in Kant's Moral and Religious Philosophy.* London: Routledge, 2003.

Munzel, G. Felicitas. *Kant's Conception of Moral Character: The 'Critical' Link of Morality, Anthropology, and Reflective Judgment.* Chicago: University of Chicago Press, 1999.

Nell, Onora (O'Neill). *Acting on Principle: An Essay on Kantian Ethics.* New York: Columbia University Press, 1975.

O'Neill, Onora. *Constructions of Reason: Explorations of Kant's Practical Philosophy.* Cambridge: Cambridge University Press, 1989.

—— *Bounds of Justice.* Cambridge: Cambridge University Press, 2000.

Reath, Andrews. *Agency and Autonomy in Kant's Moral Theory: Selected Essays*. Oxford: Clarendon Press, 2006.

Rossvær, Viggo. *Kant's Moral Philosophy: An Interpretation of the Categorical Imperative*. Oslo: Universitetsforlag, 1979.

Sherman, Nancy. *Making a Necessity of Virtue: Aristotle and Kant on Virtue*. Cambridge: Cambridge University Press, 1997.

Stratton-Lake, Philip. *Kant, Duty, and Moral Worth*. London: Routledge, 2000.

Sullivan, Roger J. *Immanuel Kant's Moral Theory*. Cambridge: Cambridge University Press, 1989.

Williams, T.C. *The Concept of the Categorical Imperative*. Oxford: Clarendon Press, 1968.

Wood, Allen W. *Kant's Ethical Thought*. Cambridge: Cambridge University Press, 1999.

6. MULTIPLE-AUTHOR ANTHOLOGIES ON KANT'S MORAL PHILOSOPHY

Chadwick, Ruth F., ed. *Immanuel Kant: Critical Assessments*. Volume III: Kant's Moral and Political Philosophy. London: Routledge, 1992.

Engstrom, Stephen and Jennifer Whiting, eds. *Aristotle, Kant, and the Stoics*. Cambridge: Cambridge University Press, 1996.

Guyer, Paul, ed. *Kant's Groundwork of the Metaphysics of Morals: Critical Essays*. Lanham: Rowman & Littlefield, 1998.

Horn, Christoph and Dieter Schöenecker, eds, *Groundwork for the Metaphysics of Morals*. Berlin and New York: Walter de Gruyter, 2006.

Klemme, Heiner F. and Manfred Kuehn, eds. *Immanuel Kant*. Volume II: Practical Philosophy. Aldershot: Ashgathe/Dartmouth, 1999.

Timmons, Mark, ed. *Kant's Metaphysics of Morals: Interpretative Essays*. Oxford: Oxford University Press, 2002.

Yovel, Yirmiahu, ed. *Kant's Practical Philosophy Reconsidered*. Dordrecht: Kluwer, 1989.

INDEX